DEFENDING
SOUTH CAROLINA'S
COAST

DEFENDING SOUTH CAROLINA'S COAST

THE CIVIL WAR FROM GEORGETOWN TO LITTLE RIVER

RICK SIMMONS

Charleston  London

THE
History
PRESS

Published by The History Press
Charleston, SC 29403
www.historypress.net

Copyright © 2009 by Rick Simmons
All rights reserved

First published 2009

Manufactured in the United States

ISBN 978.1.59629.780.7

Library of Congress Cataloging-in-Publication Data

Simmons, Rick.
Defending South Carolina's coast : the Civil War from Georgetown to Little River / Rick
Simmons.
p. cm.
Includes bibliographical references.
ISBN 978-1-59629-780-7
1. South Carolina--History--Civil War, 1861-1865. 2. United States--History--Civil
War, 1861-1865--Campaigns. 3. United States--History--Civil War, 1861-1865--Naval
operations. 4. Atlantic Coast (S.C.)--History, Military--19th century. I. Title.
E470.65.S56 2009
975.7'03--dc22
2009026254

CONTENTS

Preface   7

Chapter One. The North Island, South Island and Cat Island Forts   11
Chapter Two. "I Deemed it Prudent to Surrender rather than
     Have the Men All Shot Down": Fort Randall and Operations
     at Little River   31
Chapter Three. The Plantation War: Rice, Salt and Contrabands   47
Chapter Four. "He Was Hung Immediately after Capture":
     The Assault on Murrells Inlet   67
Chapter Five. Blockaders and Blockade Runners   85
Chapter Six. "Well-constructed, and Very Formidable": Battery
     White, Fort Wool and Frazier's Point   103
Chapter Seven. "A Vessel of War of Some Magnitude":
     The Confederate Gunboat CSS *Pee Dee*   125
Chapter Eight. The Eventful Final Days of the USS *Harvest Moon*   139

Appendix. A Timeline for Civil War–related Events from
     Georgetown to Little River   155
Bibliography   177
Index   181
About the Author   189

PREFACE

Defending South Carolina's Coast: The Civil War from Georgetown to Little River has had a long and almost tortuous two-decade history. I began this book in the early 1990s, after having published several historical articles in South Carolina–based magazines that were marketed to audiences in the Pee Dee and Grand Strand areas. At that time, I lived in Litchfield and then Surfside Beach for a number of years and became interested in local history and historical research as a result. Though at the time writing was little more than a pleasant diversion, I became increasingly convinced that I needed to write a book about the topic I found most fascinating of all: the history of the Georgetown to Little River area during the Civil War. I had discovered that there were many bits and pieces of information out there but no one authoritative source that pulled them all together. I started writing that book, but I was never quite sure whether I wanted to write a strictly academic book laden with citations and footnotes (and which no one would probably read) or a more mainstream work that the average person could understand and enjoy. I kept writing, but before I completely finished the text, I decided to go to graduate school, an undertaking that had always been a dream of mine. I earned my MA and PhD and moved to Louisiana, where I became, and am currently, a professor at Louisiana Tech University.

As my wife and I raised our children, and as I published my way to tenure and promotion, there was little time to return to those old notes I had gathered in the early 1990s. We would vacation at our family home in Pawleys Island every summer, sometimes spending as much as a month there, and during those trips I would occasionally think about the war along the Strand and visit places of interest. However, living one thousand miles away and facing the pressure of academic publication left little time for writing just for a hobby, and so my notes sat in my attic, untouched for more than a decade. Finally, after more than thirty academic publications, including a book (*Factory Lives: Four Nineteenth-Century British Working-Class Autobiographies*), I at last had the freedom to pursue the completion of the book that you see before you.

Still, it took several factors and people to get me to revive and finish this project. My sister, Julie, gave me a copy of a book about touring Civil War sites of interest in the Carolinas for Christmas one year, and at first I was worried that someone had finally gotten around to finishing the job I had started. Fortunately for me, in the book's nearly four hundred pages there were merely *eleven lines* relating to any sites of interest in the area about which I had proposed writing, and these lines offered just a brief mention of Battery White and the *Harvest Moon*. Still, I realized then that if I didn't finish my project, surely someone else would. Perhaps what really got me back on track was that in June 2008 Scott Lawrence took me, my son and my wife out boating in Winyah Bay to visit the islands. We talked about the forts on the islands and visited a few sites of interest, and those trips prompted me to pull out that old manuscript and finish it at long last. I also thank Scott for running out to snap a few updated pictures of the *Harvest Moon* and Battery White and letting me use them in this book.

Of course, my wife Sue, daughter Courtenay and son Cord have always been supportive; in fact, Cord has been my picture-taking and exploring buddy on a number of site visits. My wife's father, Bill Scaife, a renowned historian and author of several books about the Civil War, has always urged me to finish this work, and I'm glad that I was finally able to do so. My own father, mother and sister have always been supportive, and so I owe them thanks as well. Dad first read my incomplete manuscript in the 1990s, so I'm sure he's glad that all of that reading and advice didn't go to waste. I also owe a great debt of thanks to my good friend Warren Cockfield, who also lent some of his photographs to this work and who kept me updated on last minute developments with the CSS *Pee Dee*. Warren also put me in touch with Tom Kirkland, and I would like to thank Mr. Kirkland for letting me use his rare photographs of the wreck of the CSS *Pee Dee*. Finally, I'd like to thank Robin Salmon and Charlene Winkler at Brookgreen Gardens for seeing me right before this book went to press so I could tie up a few loose ends on the Laurel Hill earthworks.

There were a lot of other people who helped me locate materials for this book back in the 1990s, but after a decade and a half I have unfortunately lost or forgotten many of their names: librarians at the Georgetown, Myrtle Beach, University of South Carolina and Coastal Carolina libraries and even people who simply let me walk onto their land and take pictures at places such as Wachesaw Plantation, Fort Randall and Belle Isle. I've talked to dozens of people over the years, and again, I'm sorry that so many of those casual conversations, which at the time I thought I would never forget, have slipped away. I suppose it is also appropriate to thank the men who served along this coast during the Civil War, including my own ancestors who served in the Tenth South Carolina Regiment and the Seventh South Carolina Cavalry and who were stationed in Georgetown and Murrells Inlet. And finally, if I have overlooked anyone else who helped me over the years, know that in my heart I truly thank you for your support.

CHAPTER ONE

THE NORTH ISLAND, SOUTH ISLAND AND CAT ISLAND FORTS

Even before the Civil War, those familiar with the long stretch of South Carolina coast from Georgetown to Little River were aware that there were certain key positions that would be extremely attractive to invading Union forces should a war begin. Both Little River and Murrells Inlet had anchorage enough that they could house ships laden with goods coming in and going out, and thus those inlets could be used by Union ships, as well as by the blockade runners upon whom the economic viability of the struggling South depended. The most important area of the coast by far, however, was centered on Winyah Bay. Not only was it the location of the district's largest city in Georgetown, but the bay was also large enough that it could harbor the entire United States Navy in 1861. In addition, the bay provided access to the Black, Pee Dee, Waccamaw and Sampit Rivers, and the mouths of the North and South Santee Rivers were just below Winyah Bay as well. Consequently, whoever controlled the bay controlled Georgetown, as well as the surrounding rivers, and, by extension, also determined the viability of the local rice economy.

The Georgetown area was the largest producer of rice in America and the second-largest rice-producing area in the world, but without Winyah Bay and control of the rivers, the rice would be left to rot in the fields. Though those events would eventually transpire, in 1861 the Confederacy was determined to protect the area at all costs. In order to do so, an extensive series of fortifications was constructed in the area, the largest and most important of which were the forts on North, South and Cat Islands on Winyah Bay.

The North Island Lighthouse. *Photograph by the author.*

When the Ordinance of Secession was signed in Charleston on December 20, 1860, it was the climax to a long-developing series of events that was, to some people, inevitable. Even before the official outbreak of hostilities, companies of local militia were formed and camps of instruction were established from Georgetown to Little River. In the months that followed the signing of the ordinance, more and more companies of local militia were raised and likewise tendered their services to the state. Camps of instruction sprang up at a number of locations along the Strand, and these camps were more ubiquitous than any other form of military installation during the war. Today, only names exist for many of these camps, and names alone provide few clues about their locations. While we know that Camp Marion was about two miles out of Georgetown at White's Bridge, Camp Norman was on North Island near the lighthouse, Camp Lookout was on the coast in Murrells Inlet and Camp Magill was on the Waccamaw River, in other cases only names that shed little light on these camps' locations remain. Camp Trapier (probably at Frazier's Point later in the war), Camp Waccamaw, Camp Chestnut, Camp Harlee, Camp Middleton and others now exist as no more than footnotes in the few remaining records from the period.

In addition to the camps of instruction, even before the war the government of South Carolina encouraged citizens and municipalities to build batteries in coastal areas that were important and vulnerable. In a dispatch of May 17, 1861 (almost a full month before the hostilities officially began), from General P.G.T. Beauregard to Captain F.D. Lee of the Corps of South Carolina Engineers, Beauregard instructed Lee to head to Georgetown to inspect sites for the forts that would be built along the coast. Beauregard noted that there were already two batteries at Georgetown, but he wanted the guns at the batteries consolidated into one fort (this was never done, and within a year, there would be one additional fort there, not one fewer). Defenses were planned for the mouths of Little River, Murrells Inlet, the North and South Santee and on North Island, South Island and Cat Island.

Lieutenant Louis F. LeBleux supervised much of the engineering work in the area, and earthworks were built at a number of key locations around Winyah Bay. Though often the armament was inadequate, early in the war the Federal navy didn't seem to be willing to risk testing the range of the Confederate guns very often. After the Federals captured Port Royal on November 7, 1861, it was clear that the fortifications along the coast needed improving in order to prevent other key areas from falling into Federal hands. A new department commander was appointed to supervise the construction of defenses along the coasts of South Carolina, Georgia and northern Florida, and the man chosen was General Robert E. Lee.

Although Lee's fame as a military commander would come on the battlefields of Virginia, Maryland and Pennsylvania later in the war, in 1861 he was relatively unknown to the general public. Lee, however, was an excellent engineer and was well known for his ability to plan and construct defenses. Lee knew that areas such as Horry and Georgetown Counties were important agriculturally as well as strategically, and in this knowledge he had a subordinate who was in full agreement. As Colonel Arthur Middleton Manigault, in charge of the Georgetown-Horry district, wrote:

> *It was a matter of great importance that this region of the country should [be] preserved, for a very large portion of the rice crop of the south [is] grown on the two Santees, and on the rivers emptying into Winyah Bay,—the Pee Dee, Waccamaw, Sampit, and Black Rivers. The additional means it furnishe[s] of subsistence to our armies, [is] a matter of great consequence…even at a considerable cost.*

Lee's first task was to improve the coastal defenses, a task that he would have to do with considerably fewer troops in the area. Many troops in the militia that had been stationed along the coast had been discharged, some had their terms of enlistment expire and did not reenlist, many were transferred and many were ill and unfit for duty. In December, Manigault reported that he had fewer than one thousand men on duty in the district (just months before, Manigault had an aggregate of almost three thousand men in the district, including twenty-nine companies of infantry, six companies of cavalry and one company of artillery). In spite of these shortages of manpower, Lee had Manigault reassign his troops, improve existing fortifications and, in some cases, build new ones. Area forts outside of the Winyah Bay area included Fort Ward in Murrells Inlet and Fort Randall in Little River, and it was probably at or about this time that the earthworks at Laurel Hill and Richmond Hill were built.

In Winyah Bay, the three most important positions were at North Island, South Island and Cat Island.

The Civil War from Georgetown to Little River

THE NORTH ISLAND LIGHTHOUSE AND FORT ALSTON

North Island is undoubtedly the most colorful and arguably the most historically important area along the Grand Strand. Up until the early nineteenth century, the island was a resort area for planters seeking to escape the heat of their inland residences, much like Pawleys Island to the north. North Island is much more inaccessible than Pawleys Island, however, and today it can be reached only by boat. After a hurricane in 1822 destroyed most of the houses on the island, it was used much less often as a resort; from the Civil War on, it has frequently been in a state completely devoid of human habitation, as it is today.

Prior to the Civil War, perhaps the most important historical event to take place on North Island was the landing of the Marquis de Lafayette and Baron De Kalb on the island on June 13, 1777. Lafayette and De Kalb landed a small boat in search of a pilot for their ship so that they

North Island is littered with brick fragments from the homes that existed before the Civil War. These bricks are just beyond the dunes on North Island, on the Winyah Bay side of the island. *Photograph by the author.*

15

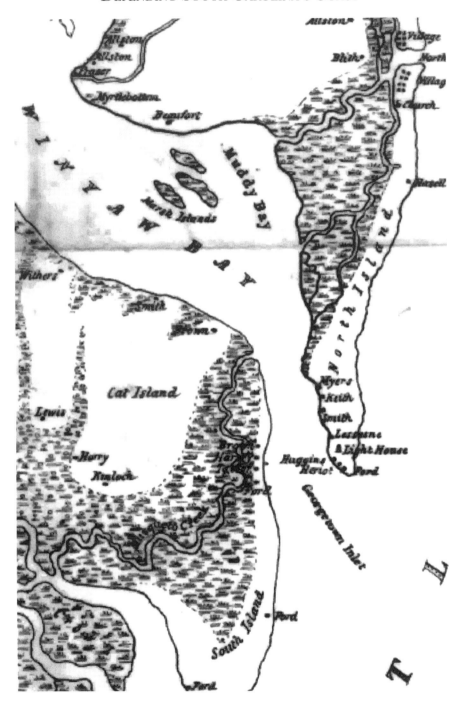

This *Mill's Atlas* map of 1825 shows the proximity of North, South and Cat Islands and establishes the degree to which forts at those locations would have controlled access to Winyah Bay. *Library of Congress Map Collection.*

could eventually join George Washington. They were brought to the North Island summer home of Benjamin Huger, where they stayed for two days before proceeding to Charleston. Today, a historical marker on Highway 17 commemorates that event.

More noteworthy and more important in terms of its bearing on the Civil War was the construction of the North Island Lighthouse, which is the oldest existing lighthouse in South Carolina and one of the oldest in the United States. Built on a tract of land donated by the planter and patriot Paul Trapier in 1789, the lighthouse was begun in 1799 and completed in 1801. This seventy-two-foot-tall structure, which was built of cyprus and burned whale oil to light its lamp, was destroyed in a storm in 1806. A second lighthouse was built on the spot by 1811, and this structure was the base for many military operations, both Union and Confederate, throughout the war.

Even early in the war, it was clear that the Georgetown lighthouse was not only important strategically but also because it provided a lookout post that was undoubtedly the highest accessible point on the coast. As a result, the main duty of troops stationed at the lighthouse was to watch for ships. As early as February 1861, mention of a redoubt named Fort Alston appears as being located on North Island, and at the beginning of the war it appears that Company D and Company B of what would become the Tenth South Carolina Regiment were stationed there in nearby Camp Norman. Unlike the other Winyah forts, no specific inventory of artillery seems to exist, but a letter dated February 22, 1861, from John R. Beaty of the Tenth South Carolina Regiment, mentions that "the cannon at Fort Alston are firing and the balls pass down the Bay…they are practicing range to be ready…it has an ugly sound but I suppose I can get used to it."

As for conditions on the island, Beaty wrote, "It is a bleak barren row of sandhills exposed to the ocean on one side and Winyah Bay on the other… covered with a thick grove of pine and palmetto, very hilly and broken and a most capital place for riflemen to skirmish." There was also, for a time in 1861, a small fort on the north end of the island (at one time companies A, E, H and K of the Tenth Regiment were alternately stationed there), though it appears that this fort did not permanently mount any artillery and was only occasionally armed with the mobile fieldpieces of the Waccamaw Light Artillery. In April 1861, Major William Capers White notes having posted Captain Thomas West Daggett, two officers and twenty-six men of the Waccamaw Light Artillery on coast watch on North Island; thus, the fort on the north end of the island may have been simply a base with some earthworks but not a major fortification.

There was clearly a need for forts on the island, not only to protect the bay but also to deal with the wrecked ships—blockade runners *and* warships—that were constantly running aground on the island. On November 2, 1861, the Union steamer *Osceola* foundered off of Georgetown, and two boats of captive crewmen were detained on North Island. On December 24, 1861, the USS *Gem of the Sea* attacked a beached runner, the *Prince of Wales*, there. That night, Colonel Manigault was informed that one thousand to fifteen hundred Union troops had landed on North Island, and though this proved to be false, the next day a Union transport ship loaded with troops passed so close to North Island that the soldiers onboard could clearly be seen by the Confederates.

Consequently, the North Island fort was important in that it sustained a Confederate presence on the island. However, when General Lee was

As this undated early twentieth-century Coast Guard photo shows, at one point there were pleasant and obviously habitable quarters on North Island for the lighthouse keepers. Today, all of these structures, save the lighthouse, have disappeared, and the area is overgrown. *U.S. Coast Guard photograph.*

transferred to more important theatres of the war, his successor, General John Pemberton, who took command on March 14, 1862, made the unpopular and controversial decision to withdraw all Confederate troops and abandon the forts in the area. He wrote to Colonel Manigault on March 25, 1862:

> *Having maturely considered the subject, I have determined to withdraw the forces from Georgetown, and therefore to abandon the position...You will proceed with all the infantry force under your command to this city, Charleston, and report to Brigadier General* [Roswell] *Ripley.*

In addition to the troop withdrawals, most of the area forts, all of which were nearly finished, were to be abandoned. Their guns were removed, transferred to railroad cars and shipped to Charleston.

Not long afterward, in May 1862, the Federals realized that the island forts were undefended, and the USS *Albatross*, commanded by George A. Prentiss, and the steamer USS *Norwich*, commanded by Lieutenant J.M. Duncan, entered Winyah Bay. The two commanders noted that when they passed North Island, the redoubt and lighthouse were deserted, as were similar forts on South and Cat Islands. Prentiss landed Union troops, and North Island was now officially in Federal hands and would remain so for the rest of the war.

The Federals made better use of the island than had the Confederates, however. After sailing into Georgetown on May 22, the *Albatross* and the *Norwich* proceeded up the Waccamaw River and raided a mill, carrying off eighty slaves in the process. The ships returned to North Island and disembarked the slaves, the first members of a "contraband" colony that was to grow quickly. Soon, hundreds of slaves began flocking to North Island, and before long more than seven hundred contrabands appear to have been under Federal protection there. The Federals were never entirely happy with this situation, as it took a considerable troop presence to protect the former slaves and utilized precious supplies to feed them. There was also great concern that the Confederates would attempt to raid the island to kill the contrabands, and Prentiss had his boats constantly shelling the woods on North, South and Cat Islands to disperse any Confederates who might try to approach the new Federal camps.

On May 25, Prentiss reported that "there is not now a solitary Rebel on North or South Island" and that, as an added protection, he had "destroyed the last remaining bridge which connects with the mainland, and there is no longer danger from incursion of cavalry, the only arm that is efficient or dares venture down here." Despite his bravado, the situation on North Island remained an uneasy one at best. In 1862, Commander I.B. Baxter of the *Gem of the Sea* noted that there were about "500 troops at Georgetown, consisting of cavalry, infantry, and artillery, who intend crossing over in boats from Georgetown to [Pawleys] Island and from thence to the north end of North Island, with the intention of destroying the contrabands." Although the intended raid never amounted to more than a rumor, by that time the colony numbered more than one thousand contrabands; later, more than seventeen hundred escaped slaves had flocked to the Federal lines. By March 1863, Admiral Samuel DuPont ordered the contraband colony removed and sent to Port Royal. This action eliminated the threat of a Confederate massacre once and for all.

The last major event of note involving North Island occurred on June 2, 1864, when the USS *Wamsutta* chased the side-wheel steamer *Rose* to ground on North Island. A Union sentry in the North Island Lighthouse spotted the ship lying close offshore near North Inlet at about 9:00 a.m., and the *Wamsutta* went in pursuit. The *Rose* ran ashore near the wreck of another steamer, and men from the *Wamsutta* boarded it. A force of about seventy-five Confederate cavalrymen came from the direction of the north end of the island. The Union sailors attempted to attach a rope from the *Rose* to the *Wamsutta* and tow it off, but the runner was firmly mired in the sand and would not budge. By this time, the *Wamsutta*'s captain noted that "the cavalry had advanced to the edge of the woods, and commenced firing at our men on board the steamer, who returned their fire, and I also shelled the woods, which kept them back." Rather than have any valuable supplies fall into Confederate hands, the Federals burned the *Rose*. Nevertheless, as late as June 9, Confederates were reported attempting to salvage machinery from the wreck.

Despite the fact that the North Island redoubt was of no real importance as a fort, the lighthouse and the island's location at the mouth of Winyah Bay ensured that the position would always be of interest to both sides, and North Island was the Federals' major land base of operations along the Strand until Georgetown surrendered in

1865. As the Confederate forces in Georgetown faced further reductions in troops, little thought was given to trying to regain a foothold on North Island. The lighthouse was also burned during the war and had to be at least partially rebuilt in 1867, providing the basis of the structure that exists today.

THE SOUTH ISLAND AND CAT ISLAND FORTS

Because of their proximity, the forts on the north side of South and Cat Islands could be clearly seen by each other. However, South Island had the distinction of having two forts: one on its north side, overlooking Winyah Bay, and one on its south side, guarding the mouth of the North Santee River. This latter fort was planned as a five-gun battery overlooking the Santee from the south end of South Island, and at times companies C, G, I, L and M of the Tenth South Carolina were stationed there while it was under construction. By November 1861, Colonel Manigault was ready to garrison the fort, although only three twelve-pounders were in place. Eventually, however, this fort was abandoned, without ever having been fully armed, and its guns were transferred to Cat Island. At various periods throughout the war, attempts would be made to refortify the position, but it appears that it was never practical to do so. Other than deploying skirmishers there to harass Union sailors on ships attempting to enter the Santee, it never seems to have been a viable defensive position.

The fort on the north side of the island overlooking Winyah Bay was an important position early in the war. In November 1861, this fort had four twenty-four-pounders, one rifled six-pounder and one eighteen-pounder. Like the Cat Island fort, this position had three faces and an open rear, along with a bombproof. In addition, this position protected two nearby Confederate hospitals. Other than the hospitals, the fort apparently never saw much use, and it is only rarely mentioned in the Confederate correspondence of the period. The fort's most prominent notice came after its abandonment by the Confederates, as it is mentioned in the May 21, 1862 reports of the USS *Albatross* and the steamer USS *Norwich*. Passing the island, they could see "quite an extensive fortification, with apparently several large guns mounted en

This page: Of the seven nineteenth-century artillery pieces found in Georgetown today, the history of only two remains elusive. While records definitely place five of the guns at Battery White, this twenty-four-pound naval gun, found in the Sampit River in 1991, is of obscure origin. While it may have been lost in the river even before the war, it is possible that it could have been one of the antiquated guns that Beauregard ordered relocated in 1861 or one of the guns that Pemberton had removed from the district in 1862 (the South Island and Cat Island forts had twenty-four-pounders in place early in the war). *Photograph by the author.*

barbette," though on closer inspection they saw that the fort was deserted and that the cannons were actually Quaker guns (logs painted to look like artillery) because the Confederates had removed the guns when they retreated into Georgetown.

Its sister fort on Cat Island was without a doubt the largest and most impressive fort on Winyah Bay during the early part of the war and was probably second only to Battery White when one considers all of the forts built along the Strand during the conflict. The Cat Island fort was likely one of the two original forts at Winyah Bay mentioned in General Beauregard's prewar dispatch cited earlier, and whatever plans Beauregard may have had for dismantling the fort, General Lee disregarded them. A letter from Colonel Manigault dated November 15, 1861, notes that the fort at Cat Island was still unfinished, with the "three principal faces nearly completed" but no bombproof. The fort did, however, mount two thirty-two-pounders, one rifled twelve-pounder and two twenty-four-pounders at that time. In December, when work on the battery on the North Santee was abandoned, the three twelve-pounders at that battery were also sent to Cat Island.

The troops stationed on Cat Island of course changed throughout the war, and apparently for a number of reasons Cat Island was considered a preferable station to some of the other forts in the area. John R. Beaty of the Tenth South Carolina wrote in December 1861:

> *I had rather be stationed at the Cat Island Fort, than the South Island fort, for several reasons. One is that it is a better place to winter, there is plenty of wood…Cat Island is only divided from the mainland by a narrow creek easy to cross in case it becomes necessary to abandon the island to fight on the mainland.*

Not only was the fort well armed, but it was also easily defensible, as engineers cut down all of the timber within one thousand yards of the fort in order to provide a clear field of fire. In addition, the men were apparently able to build their own huts there, and Beaty's hut had "a good shingle roof with a roaring fire in a brick chimney with a table."

In other ways, though, living conditions there apparently were not good. For the Confederate soldiers stationed in the district, life at the island forts offered little diversion from the daily routine of drilling, drilling

Passing by the Cat Island fort today, one can see the remains of the massive earthworks that housed Confederate troops and artillery. The Cat Island fort effectively protected Winyah Bay until it was ordered abandoned by General Pemberton in 1862. *Photograph by the author.*

and more drilling. Besides the boredom, the soldiers had to deal with the uncomfortable surroundings in which they were forced to live. Beaty wrote from Cat Island in January:

> *I am greatly at a loss to know why this place is called Cat Island. It worries me sometimes till I can't sleep. Why there ain't a cat on it, and it don't look like there ever was….Now if they had called it Flea Island, then I'd have understood it. My very legs understand the very meaning of the word flea…I never saw such whoppers. They make ridges on top of the ground like moles only not quite so large…There is a creek about a half a mile from the fort called Misquito Creek and I can understand that too. Such busters and so numerous, they can sing "Dixie" almost as good as the negroes that are at work on the fort.*

In February 1862, sickness among the troops reached alarming proportions. Beaty noted on February 6 that during the preceding four days, disease had killed an average of two men a day in his regiment. So often were the men sick from disease (smallpox was also raging in Georgetown, with twenty-four cases reported in February) that later, when Lee left the area and needed troops for his army in May 1862, he told Pemberton that he might as well send the Georgetown-based troops to him because "the troops that you retain there will suffer more from disease than the enemy." The susceptibility to disease was no doubt aided by the paucity of the soldiers' diets, which would become an all-too-common occurrence in the years ahead. "We are living exactly hard here," Beaty wrote. "Our daily food is rice and salt beef boiled together, crackers without salt, and our drink is sassafras tea sweetened with molasses." There would come a time when Beaty and many other Confederate soldiers would see even these bland rations as sumptuous.

Like the forts at North and South Islands, the Cat Island fort was never called upon to repel a Federal attack, and it was only after Pemberton stripped the area defenses in 1862 that the Federals had their first good look at the fort. Commander Prentiss of the *Albatross* reported in May 1862, after the fort was abandoned, that it was "a well-built fortification of quadrangular form, fitted with platforms for mounting ten guns and containing bombproofs, magazine, and furnace for hot shot." The guns had of course been removed. Even though the fort had been abandoned, "some cavalry appeared in the skirts of the woodland," and Prentiss noted that "we scattered them with a few shells." Prentiss landed some men and burned the wooden portions of the forts, terminating its usefulness as a defensive position.

Thus, by May 1862, the Cat Island fort, like the other forts in Winyah Bay, was in Federal hands. On several occasions later in the war, the Federals noted that Confederate sharpshooters would sneak into the earthworks and take shots at the Union sailors on their ships. As a military outpost, however, the fort would never again be used.

THE ISLANDS TODAY

Today, the land on North, South and Cat Islands is a part of the Tom Yawkey Wildlife Preserve. The Yawkey Preserve encompasses roughly thirty-one square miles of protected island land, and while this has kept the land from being developed, it also means that it is largely off-limits to the public.

The beach on North Island. *Photograph by the author.*

North Island today is so large that it staggers the mind to see such a massive pristine tract of undeveloped coastal property. The island is lush and overgrown with vegetation, and though everywhere there are minute remnants of man's former presence (see the picture of the bricks earlier in this chapter), the island is devoid of human life, and it is easy to forget that anyone ever did live there.

In one place only has man made a discernable ecological footprint on the island, and that is near the easternmost point on the Winyah Bay side of the island, where the remains of the Georgetown lighthouse station stand. The lighthouse that stands today was built in 1867; it is eighty-seven feet tall, with a base diameter of twenty feet and a wall thickness of six inches. Though the original buildings in the early twentieth-century picture included earlier in this chapter have all vanished, at some point a bunkhouse and other structures were built to house the Coast Guard attendants stationed on the island. The Coast Guard automated the light in 1986 and abandoned the station at that time. About two years later, the Department of Juvenile Justice established a marine rehabilitation program for juvenile offenders on the island, but the

The Cat Island earthworks as seen from Winyah Bay. *Photograph by the author.*

An abandoned structure near the pier, North Island. *Photograph by the author.*

The abandoned Coast Guard station at North Island. *Photograph by the author.*

program was eventually discontinued. Facilities on the island have now rapidly deteriorated, and the buildings sit isolated and abandoned.

Conditions on South Island are a bit different, if only because the base facilities for the Yawkey Preserve are located on South and Cat Islands, so those places have a slightly more active human population, small though it may be. Even from the water, it is obvious that there are several structures on the island and that they are inhabited or at least well maintained.

The earthworks on Cat Island are most impressive. Time and the forces of nature have eroded the shoreline to the point that, at high tide, the fort is very near the waterline. The size of the earthworks is even today quite remarkable; there is no mistaking that this was a fort and that each part of it was well built for its intended purpose.

CHAPTER TWO

"I DEEMED IT PRUDENT TO SURRENDER RATHER THAN HAVE THE MEN ALL SHOT DOWN"

Fort Randall and Operations at Little River

Of the many Confederate forts, camps and batteries built during the Civil War along what is today known as the Grand Strand, two necessitate having their stories told in detail because of the intricacy of their construction, their strategic importance to the Union and the Confederacy, or both. The first built of the two, Fort Randall at Little River Inlet, was the northernmost fortification on the Grand Strand and stood isolated roughly forty miles from the nearest Confederate outpost. As such, it was intended to be practically self-sufficient.

Despite its isolation, Little River was important because not only were the docks an ideal place for loading and unloading ships' supplies, but also extensive saltworks located nearby provided much-needed salt for preserving meat bound for soldiers at the front lines. In addition, although Little River Inlet could not house a flotilla of ships as could Winyah Bay to the south, and although it did not provide access to numerous inland targets and plantations as did the rivers below Georgetown, it was still important strategically. Due to its proximity to the Confederate stronghold Fort Fisher in Wilmington, and because of its near centrality between Wilmington and Charleston, Little River was in a key position. As a result, Fort Randall and Little River Inlet would be the site of a number of skirmishes, encounters between Federal gunboats and Confederate blockade runners and several daring raids by the Union navy.

The government of South Carolina planned and built a system of coastal defenses intended to protect the agriculturally rich areas of Horry and Georgetown Counties in the event of hostilities. Because of the region's system of rivers providing access to the interior of the state, once the war commenced the area was considered of prime importance not only to natives of South Carolina but also to the Confederacy as a whole. Plans called for fortifications to be built north of the district at Little River, in the center at Murrells Inlet, in the south at the mouths of the North and South Santee Rivers and on North, South and Cat Islands.

In 1861, Colonel Arthur Middleton Manigault (later to be promoted to brigadier general) of the Tenth Regiment, South Carolina Volunteers, was named commander of what was then known as the First Military District, which encompassed the defenses from the North Carolina line to the South Santee River. Because Confederate officials believed that South Carolina would first be invaded either at Hilton Head or Georgetown (the Union's object being a harbor in the proximity of its ultimate target: well-defended Charleston Harbor), Manigault had a coastal defense force at his disposal numbering twenty-nine companies of infantry, six companies of cavalry and one company of artillery, in addition to a number of home-guard units serving in the district. This gave Manigault an aggregate of almost three thousand men, a sizable amount by the day's standards and the largest military force stationed in the area at any time during the war. Although the number of troops in the area would decrease quickly (the Federals seized Hilton Head in November 1861, and Manigault's force was reduced to one thousand men by December), Manigault and the succeeding commanders of the district nevertheless had to find ways to garrison the district's most important defensive positions, even though their troops were spread thin.

The anchor on the north end of the district was the battery at the mouth of Little River, and logistically, the site for what would come to be known as Fort Randall was well chosen and easily defendable. Situated on Tilghman's Point, a slight bluff overlooking Little River Inlet, the position offered a commanding view of the land and sea that revealed anything approaching for miles. The primary fortification was a wooden blockhouse surrounded by concealing earthworks, all of which were enclosed by a moat ten feet wide and five feet deep. Although these features made the fort easily defendable, more formidable were the cannons that the fort held in 1861. The Confederate objective early in the war was to build coastal strongholds and stock them with artillery pieces that would not only defend the district if needed but would also deter the Federal forces probing the

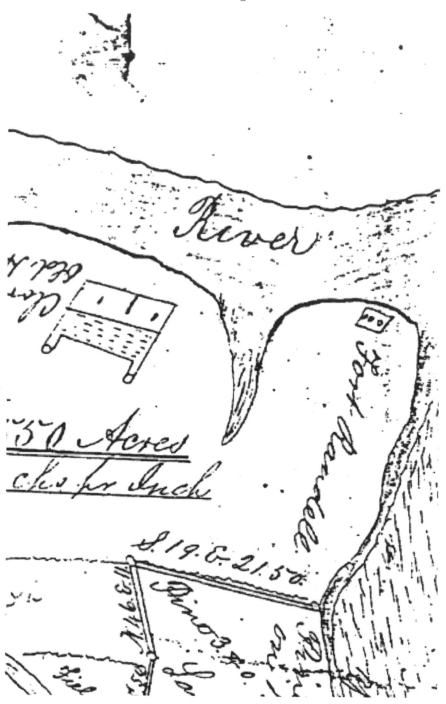

A portion of a deed dated November 1862. The deed registers ownership of the 550 acres containing Fort Randall and the Clardy house to Thomas Randall.

area if they felt inclined to invade. Consequently, in 1861, Fort Randall's four artillery pieces—two six-pounders and two twelve-pounders—were comparable in number to the seaside batteries on the southern end of the coast on Winyah Bay and at Fort Ward in Murrells Inlet.

Because Fort Randall was the only major fortification on the north end of the coast early in the war, it is not surprising that the *Horry Dispatch* reported that the dedication ceremony in 1861 was an occasion of considerable fanfare, attended and presided over by local military luminaries such as Major William Capers White, Captain Thomas Randall, Captain J. Litchfield, Lieutenant L.L. Clements and Lieutenant T.W. Gore. According to a dispatch from Major White to the Confederate secretary of war, dated April 13, 1861, just one day after the hostilities officially began at Fort Sumter, the first Confederate troops officially posted at Fort Randall were thirty-three men and three officers from Captain Litchfield's All Saints Riflemen. Once the situation in the area stabilized, Major White served as the fort's first commanding officer, and the men in his command (from the Seventh South Carolina Infantry) manned Fort Randall until they were transferred out of the district and attached to the regular Confederate army.

The unit most frequently stationed at the fort during the war was the ubiquitous Waccamaw Light Artillery, initially under the command of Captain Thomas West Daggett and later under the command of Georgetown planter Joshua John Ward (and then others) after Daggett joined the Tenth South Carolina Regiment in the regular Confederate army. In addition, "coast guard" patrols, though not stationed at Fort Randall, were often deployed and shuffled from one area to another as needed. The first of these assigned to support Fort Randall was composed of forty-three men and three officers of Captain T.F. Gillespie's Carolina Greys, which was responsible for patrolling the forty-mile area from Murrells Inlet to Little River in April 1861. Another unit that periodically fought in support of the troops at Fort Randall was the Camden Mounted Rifles under the command of Captain A.H. Boykin. The Camden troops greatly relieved the pressure on the thinly spread Confederate regulars in the district, and Boykin's men patrolled the beaches as far north as Little River, ultimately even relieving Fort Randall during emergencies.

As the war continued, however, trying to allocate the diminishing numbers of troops to the numerous forts along the Grand Strand proved impossible, and most of the first-built forts were dismantled within two years. Once Hilton Head capitulated, the Confederates considered a Federal invasion of the district unlikely, and therefore the forts in Horry and Georgetown Counties were no longer considered key strategic posts. Consequently, twenty of the guns from the area forts were summarily stripped and sent up the Pee Dee River to the Northeastern Railroad bridge and then transferred to railroad cars and shipped to Charleston. The guns were not the only things to go, however, as most of the forts in Horry and Georgetown Counties were de-garrisoned, and the troops were sent to Charleston and other theatres of the war.

Of the original forts built along the coast, only Fort Randall remained manned on a regular basis, but even there the artillery had been removed. Unwilling to leave the area so obviously undefended, however, the cannons at the abandoned forts, including Fort Randall, were replaced with logs painted black to give them the appearance of artillery pieces. Called "Quaker guns," these made it appear that the installations were still heavily fortified. Yet even though it was still manned, the situation at Fort Randall was dire. Whereas in Georgetown troops could be shuffled back and forth between positions in a matter of hours when reinforcements were needed, when Federal incursions made Fort Randall untenable—as they soon would—support troops might take a day or more to arrive, if they arrived at all. The troops around Georgetown were often better supplied and better armed, and indeed, when Battery White in Georgetown was built it had anywhere from nine to sixteen guns in place at any time from 1863 on. Fort Randall had been completely stripped of artillery by that same year.

Remarkably, at first the Union navy didn't know how vulnerable the fort was, and even if it suspected, it still showed the fort a healthy respect. One of the first official Federal military accounts mentioning activity of any type in the vicinity of Fort Randall was a report by Lieutenant George W. Browne of the USS *Fernandina*. Browne reported that on December 13, 1861, he witnessed what he believed to be more than forty signal fires along the coast at Little River, which he judged were guides for a blockade runner or runners attempting to come in. Based on the number of men he saw when he ran in closer to shore, he realized that "there was an encampment of Confederate troops and the distant fires were their picket guard." Browne explained that he opened fire with his starboard artillery and that in the darkness he could hear his shells strike some hard surface. He said he came around and fired on the Confederate troops again with shell and grapeshot. By this time, apparently, the Confederates had dispersed, and Browne moved back out to sea.

Browne did not, however, try and run under the fort's guns, though he must have thought it odd that Fort Randall's artillery had not returned the *Fernandina*'s fire. He, of course, had no way of knowing that the fort's guns were just Quaker guns, and Union naval records show that it was only after Federal gunboats decided to mount an assault on the Georgetown island positions in May 1862 that they realized the artillery had been removed from the area batteries. Once the Union navy suspected that Fort Randall, like other area defenses, had no artillery, there was little to stop it from attacking Little River, and it acted fairly quickly. On June 25, 1862, six Union boats—one each from the USS *Penobscot*, the USS *Mystic*, the USS *Mount Vernon* and the USS *Victoria* and two from the USS *Monticello*—entered the inlet and went eight miles up to the town of Little River to destroy some blockade runners reported to be there.

The citizens of Little River fled when the Union boats approached, so the Federals worked unhindered as they destroyed two schooners, sixty bales of cotton, two hundred barrels of turpentine and fifty-three barrels of rosin. For several months, no further landings occurred, and the Union navy seemed content to blockade the area with only an occasional foray upriver, such as when, on November 24, 1862, the *Monticello* bombarded and destroyed two extensive saltworks near Little River Inlet. However, on December 30, 1862, runaway slaves taken aboard the USS *Victoria* informed the Federals that two blockade runners, the *Argyle* and the *James Bailey*, were anchored at Little River and ready to run out. A reconnaissance party from the *Victoria* attempted to land near the town to verify this information on December 31, but they encountered a patrol of Confederate cavalry from Fort Randall and were forced to retreat to their boats. They then proceeded upriver and attempted another landing, but they once again stumbled on Confederate pickets and were forced to withdraw.

By this time, the Union navy was taking a keen interest in Little River, but interestingly enough, the Confederates still considered the anchorage a well-kept secret. In response to an October 1862 report by Confederate Charles Ost in which Ost lamented the lack of safe ports between Georgetown and Cape Fear, Major A.B. Magruder suggested Little River, as it "is not down on the charts nor on the coast survey, and its existence even—certainly its harbor and anchorage ground—is hardly known to any Yankee." One Yankee who did know about the anchorage at Little River was about to lead an assault on Fort Randall, and though unsuccessful, his efforts would point out the vulnerability of the fort and lead to further Union forays into the area.

On the evening of January 5, 1863, twenty-five men led by twenty-year-old Lieutenant William Barksdale Cushing approached the fort in three small cutters from the disguised blockade runner *Home* and the USS *Matthew Vassar*. Only nineteen years old when the war began, Cushing was the youngest man to achieve almost every rank that he held during the war. After starting the war as a master's mate in May 1861, he was made a lieutenant in July 1862 and was promoted to lieutenant commander in October 1864. During the war, Cushing was at many of the most famous naval engagements on the East Coast, and by 1863, he had already been at the Battles of Fort Hatteras and Fort Clark in 1861 and at the battle between the *Monitor* and the *Merrimac* in 1862. His greatest fame would come after 1863, with the successful sinking of the Confederate ironclad *Albemarle* in 1864, a nearly successful attempt to capture Confederate General Louis Hebert and numerous raids on Confederate forts in North Carolina, among them Fort Caswell, Fort Shaw and Fort Campbell. Cushing's accomplishments saw him promoted to commander by war's end, and he received the personal thanks of the United States Congress for his role in the *Albemarle* affair. Cushing's daring and bravado made him well suited for the task of attacking Fort Randall, and on this occasion he would not disappoint.

Lieutenant Cushing and his men approached Fort Randall in their boats, and when they were about two hundred yards away, the Confederates spotted them and let out a volley of rifle fire. Cushing beached his boats and decided that his best course of action would be to form his men in a line of battle. With their bayonets drawn and mounted, Cushing and his men charged the fort and, as he would later claim, "yell[ed] like demons." Without firing a shot, the Federals stormed the works, as Cushing noted, "going over one side as [the Confederates] escaped over the other." Initially, the rout was complete, as the surprised Confederates—a force Cushing perhaps optimistically claimed was "five times our numbers"—fled the fort while the Federals took possession of the wooden blockhouse. Cushing reported that the Confederates "left in such haste that their stores, clothing,

William Barksdale Cushing was at many of the most famous naval engagements on the East Coast, and he was even present at an important nonmilitary event: the reading of Lincoln's Gettysburg Address in 1863. Cushing achieved the rank of commander in 1872, making him the youngest officer of that rank in the U.S. Navy. Despite his fearlessness and the appearance of invincibility he displayed time and time again, Commander Cushing's health rapidly deteriorated after the war. He died in the Government Hospital for the Insane in December 1874. He was thirty-two years old. *U.S. Navy Historical Center photograph.*

ammunition, and a portion of their arms were captured." Cushing's men ate a hearty meal of pork and greens that the Confederates had left behind, destroyed what they could not take with them and proceeded upriver. Later, Captain Boykin arrived with 125 men who had been stationed at Vaught's saltworks. The two forces briefly skirmished before the greatly outnumbered Federals ran out of ammunition, and Cushing had no alternative but to return to his ship.

Although their mission had been temporarily successful, the end result of the assault on Fort Randall was that the Confederates realized how vulnerable the position was and thereafter strengthened their defenses at the fort. But the failure to take the fort also served as a lesson for Lieutenant Cushing, who did not forget the setback and who would one day visit Little River again.

Less than a month later, on February 9, reconnaissance boats from the USS *Maratanza* captured a Confederate supply boat heading for Fort Randall. The boat was manned by five Confederate soldiers, and although three of them escaped before the boat was captured, the remaining two men provided the Federals with some very valuable information. James Gainey and George Smith, the Federal ensigns in command of the Federal boats, reported that they were told that there was one company of cavalry and one company of infantry now stationed at Fort Randall, totaling 175 men. The Federals were also in possession of some badly needed Confederate supplies headed for the fort: five rifles, a dozen blankets and twenty-three each uniform jackets, pants, shirts, hats, pairs of socks and pairs of shoes—supplies that the Confederates could ill-afford to lose. But if the Federals had any intention of pursuing the three escaped Confederates, they were quickly dissuaded. Ensign Gainey noted that the escapees had by now alerted the troops at Fort Randall, "as we saw by their firing muskets and rockets." The information about the additional troops at the fort apparently served to convince the Federals that it was not a good time to try and retake the newly-reinforced fort.

That didn't stop them, however, from probing the area, although one expedition in March 1863 almost resulted in disaster. On the third of that month, the USS *Matthew Vassar*'s Hugh H. Savage sighted a large boat beached near the inlet and ordered Acting Master's Mate George Drain to take a party of seven men to destroy it. This was done easily enough, but as the landing party started back, it inexplicably turned its boat around and started to head up the inlet. Savage ordered a recall sounded, but Drain's party paid it no heed and proceeded up past Fort Randall.

Savage was confused and would soon become even more confused. Lookouts on the ship had spotted Confederate troops coming out of Fort Randall, at which time Drain and his men had landed near the fort. Savage noted that he

> *fired two guns to call his attention to the boat's recall, and likewise to drive the rebels out of the woods where* [Drain] *was, all of which he took no notice of, but proceeded with his men into the woods, where I lost sight of them, and have neither heard nor seen anything of them since.*

At this point, Savage realized that his men had been captured by the Confederates, and indeed, the next day Savage saw Drain's boat "with a quantity of Rebels in her," at whom he lobbed shells to drive them out of the boat.

The USS *Maratanza* was a side-wheel steamer armed with four twenty-four-pounders, one one-hundred-pound Parrot rifle and one nine-inch pivot smoothbore. It served most of the war attached to the North Atlantic Blockading Squadron along the coast of North Carolina. *U.S. Navy Historical Center photograph.*

Once again, Federal troops that had landed in the vicinity of Fort Randall had met with failure, but on this occasion there were repercussions. Captain Benjamin F. Sands of the USS *Dacotah* was so incensed at the capture of Drain and the men from the *Matthew Vassar*—under circumstances "so unaccountable…that it looks to me very like a desertion, or at best an act of recklessness without apparent object, and a great want of ordinary prudence and caution"—that he ordered the *Matthew Vassar* be relieved of duty in the area. A further twist on the story occurred on March 7, when the USS *Chocura* was sent to Fort Randall and reported that another ship stationed in the area, the USS *Victoria*, noted "a large number of men in the fort…with a large flag flying and much cheering." The *Victoria* began shelling the fort, forcing the Confederates out, at which time a Union sailor who had been concealed in the woods ran out onto the beach and signaled that he wanted to be picked up. This man was a member of the *Vassar*'s crew who had escaped capture and claimed that the reason the *Vassar*'s

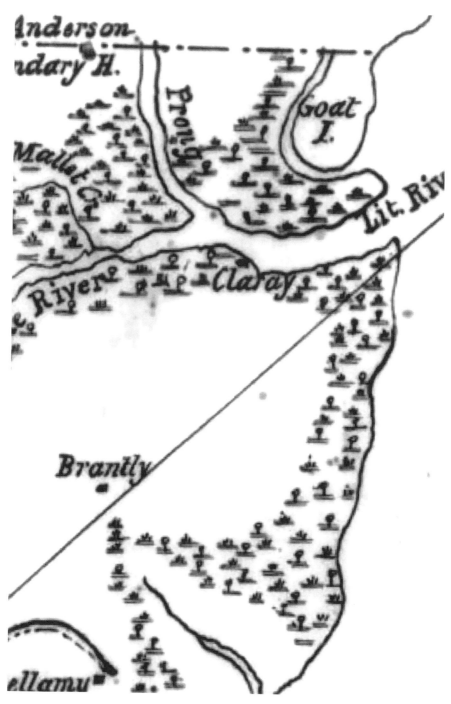

A map from the *Mill's Atlas* of 1825 shows Little River Inlet from the ocean. Fort Randall would be built on the Clardy property at center. *Library of Congress Map Collection.*

boat had landed was in order to kill a cow for food. When the Confederates surprised them, Drain ordered his men to surrender. In order to avoid capture, the sailor dove into the river, swam to the other side and hid in the marsh. Captain Sands reported that the captured crew from the *Vassar*'s boat had been sent to Fort Caswell in North Carolina and would eventually be sent to Richmond to be confined as prisoners of war.

Later, after his release from captivity, Drain claimed that his boat had been grounded on an oyster bed and that he was surprised by the Confederates. Because his men had "no sidearms or bayonets, and but ten spare cartridges for their rifles," Drain said he "deemed it prudent to surrender rather than have the men all shot down." Whatever the circumstances of Drain's and the *Vassar*'s failures, once again the Federals had suffered setbacks when up against the Confederates at Fort Randall.

Perhaps frustrated by their failure to simply drive away the Confederates at the fort, or because their attempts to have men in boats slip by or take the fort often resulted in disaster, for roughly the next year the Union ships stationed in the area contented themselves with blockading Little River and stopping the blockade runners moving in and out of the area. Even before Cushing's and Drain's expeditions, the Union ships had encountered a number of blockade runners in early 1863, although those encounters had met with a mixed rate of success. The *Victoria* had captured the schooner *Argyle* on January 2, 1863, but the runner *James Bailey* was able to slip away in the confusion. The schooner *Florida* had been captured on January 11, while on the night of February 20, the *Matthew Vassar* had fired a volley across a blockade runner's bow, but the ship had disappeared into the darkness. On February 22, the *Matthew Vassar* and the *Victoria* reported barely missing a steamer running out of the inlet and that later that same night, a runner trying to enter the inlet saw the two Union ships on blockading duty and returned to the high seas.

While these near misses must have been frustrating for the Federals, perhaps the most frustrating encounter of all came on the night of February 24. A steamer trying to run into Little River came upon a patrolling Federal guard boat from the *Matthew Vassar*. Someone on the steamer hailed the soldiers in the guard boat, undoubtedly because they were unable to determine if they were friend or foe in the darkness. The Federals in the boat replied that they were Confederates and asked the runner's name, which, according to the Union sailors, was given as either *Hero* or *Arrow*. The Federals then shouted that they were coming aboard, and when they were within twenty-five yards of the ship, they made a dash for the runner and tried to board it.

Realizing that it was a trap, the captain of the runner tried to escape, at which time the Federal soldiers in the boat launched a volley of rifle and small arms fire fore and aft of the runner and ordered it to stop. Nevertheless, the captain of the steamer opted instead for his freedom and renewed his attempt to escape. At this time, the *Matthew Vassar* came up in support and fired a broadside at the steamer, joined by the crew of the small boat, which fired two more volleys. The daring captain of the runner headed for the high seas, and owing to the *Matthew Vassar*'s distance from the runner and the exhaustion of the crew of the small boat, the steamer was able to slip out to sea. The captain of the *Matthew Vassar* signaled to the *Victoria* to take up the chase, but it, too, was unable to catch the runner.

The *Victoria* fared better in March, when, on the twenty-first, it sighted a side-wheel steamer attempting to run the blockade. The *Victoria* and the *William Bacon* went in pursuit, eventually firing half a dozen shots at the ship in order to make it heel to. When the steamer pulled up, it hoisted the British flag and, upon boarding, proved to be the *Nicolai I*, a blockade runner out of Nassau—though now a Union prize.

Little River was certainly no longer "hardly known to any Yankee," and in fact the blockade tightened; there were fewer and fewer actions of note in the area other than an occasional report of a blockade runner captured or destroyed. Perhaps the Federals felt that Little River was sealed up well enough at this point that they simply needed to wait the Confederates out, and obviously, as a fort without any artillery and few troops, Fort Randall didn't present a formidable bastion that needed to be conquered in order to win the war. From 1863 on, most of the more significant engagements in the area occurred to the south of Fort Randall and Little River. Vaught's saltworks at Withers Swash in what is now Myrtle Beach was the scene of significant destruction, and Murrells Inlet was the target of a Federal landing and bombardment. Most of the attention of the Union navy in the district was drawn to the newly built Battery White on Winyah Bay, which, according to Union Admiral John Dahlgren, was "a very formidable work" mounting sixteen guns. In light of these more pressing targets, Little River, which was relatively well bottled up by 1864, received very little attention from the Federals. By that same year, even the Confederate troops had apparently been removed from Fort Randall, as the Confederates seemed to realize the futility

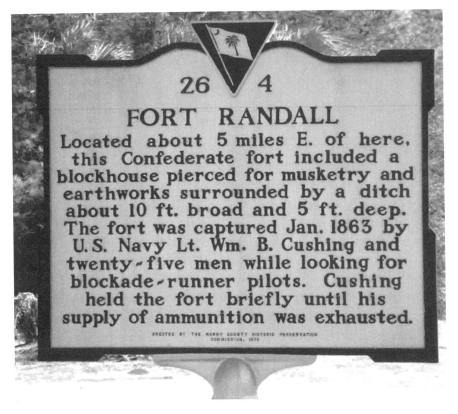

26 ▽ 4

FORT RANDALL
Located about 5 miles E. of here, this Confederate fort included a blockhouse pierced for musketry and earthworks surrounded by a ditch about 10 ft. broad and 5 ft. deep. The fort was captured Jan. 1863 by U. S. Navy Lt. Wm. B. Cushing and twenty-five men while looking for blockade-runner pilots. Cushing held the fort briefly until his supply of ammunition was exhausted.

ERECTED BY THE HORRY COUNTY HISTORIC PRESERVATION COMMISSION, 1978

The Fort Randall historical marker, Little River. *Photograph by the author.*

of manning a nearly defenseless and significantly less-important position than Georgetown when troops were desperately needed elsewhere.

By 1865, however, mopping-up operations were beginning as the war wound to its inevitable close. Since the fall of Wilmington's Fort Fisher on January 15, the ships and men serving in the North Atlantic Blockading Squadron had been able to turn their attention to the smaller areas still in Confederate hands, and the Federals saw Little River as a piece of unfinished business. The man chosen to finally subdue Little River was Lieutenant William Cushing, and again he was to lead a small party of men into an enemy position—though this mission would be far more successful than the assault on Fort Randall in 1863.

On February 5, Cushing took fifty men in four boats from the *Monticello* and went up to the town of Little River. His men easily captured the

The Civil War from Georgetown to Little River

town, as the few Confederates to be found there readily surrendered. After securing the town, his men destroyed an estimated $15,000 worth of cotton that was sitting on the wharves and slated to be shipped out. While his men occupied the town, he had occasion to meet some of the area citizens, and his observations about their attitudes were interesting. "The South Carolina planters, and all men whom I met, professed to be willing to come back under the old government," Cushing wrote, "and most of them seemed to be loyal men, only awaiting the emancipation from military rule." In any event, Little River and Fort Randall were now in Federal hands, and so it seems that the local residents had their wishes granted.

FORT RANDALL TODAY

Today, Fort Randall's relative isolation is perhaps more apparent than ever. Not only does it sit at the northernmost end of the Grand Strand, far

This page and next: All that exists at the site of Fort Randall today are the gently sloping mounds that were once part of the wall around the blockhouse. The earthworks have eroded over the years, but as these pictures attest, any Federal ships approaching Little River would have been spotted by troops at Fort Randall long before they were close enough to mount an assault. *Photographs by the author.*

from the bustle of most tourists and the places they visit, but also the fact that it sits on private property makes it all but inaccessible. A historical marker on Highway 17 notes that the fort's location is approximately five miles to the east, and because the remains of the fort are now little more than gently sloping ripples in the landscape, there is little to see even if the visitor stands in the midst of what was once the blockhouse. What is most disconcerting is that over the past decade or so the site has actually fallen victim to severe erosion and is in danger of eventually collapsing into the inlet. However, even today the view from Tilghman's Point is magnificent, and it is easy to see why it was chosen as a site for the fort. The position offers a commanding view of the land and sea that reveals anything approaching for miles.

CHAPTER THREE

THE PLANTATION WAR

Rice, Salt and Contrabands

To examine the events that transpired along the Grand Strand during the Civil War and see them merely as a series of conflicts at places such as Murrells Inlet, Battery White and Fort Randall, or as principally a naval war involving the likes of the USS *Harvest Moon* and the CSS *Pee Dee*, is to grossly oversimplify the situation. For the Confederates, the mission was not only to defend the district but also to keep rice and salt production up and goods moving in and out of Horry and Georgetown Counties. For the Federals, it was a matter of keeping the area blockaded and eventually forcing the local populace into economic submission, thus crushing their will to fight. This accounts, in part, for why there were so few large-scale invasions of the area; burning a rice mill, destroying a saltworks or taking in runaway slaves were as effective actions as an invasion of one thousand troops and would be far less costly in every sense of the word. In short, the economic war, where the stakes were rice, salt and slaves, was central to the conflict as it existed along the Grand Strand during the Civil War.

This war centered not on the coastal fortifications but on the rivers, plantations and saltworks that provided the backbone of the economy in the district. There were forts, encampments and batteries constructed on the rivers at plantations such as Richmond Hill, Laurel Hill and Sparkman's Plantation, and saltworks at places such as Little River and Singleton's Swash were often protected by Confederate blockhouses and manned by troops as well. These locations find their way into the annals of local history on a number of occasions and were actually the sites of far more action than the larger, better-known and better-defended Confederate fortifications that still partially exist today. Some were built before the war began, as area plantation owners exhibited the same perspicacity that they had when raising local militia units even before the formal secession of South Carolina from the Union. Those with foresight knew that if the plantations and saltworks were protected and the slaves could work unhindered, rice and salt production could go on and the South would remain economically viable. As a result, the economic importance of the area was foreseen very early in the war.

By 1861, impressive fortifications had been built at locations up and down the coast. The district was well fortified not only because the area was home to a number of wealthy and influential people whose produce was of economic importance to the Confederacy, but also because the Black Pee Dee, Waccamaw and Sampit Rivers all flowed into Winyah Bay. Consequently, whichever military force occupied Georgetown had control of these rivers, as well as the North and South Santee Rivers to some degree, and could exercise a great degree of control in South Carolina.

Nevertheless, the area's principal attraction, as Union General Daniel Hunter wrote in May 1862, was that "there is said to be 4,000,000 or 5,000,000 bushels [of rice there]. It is important that we should have this rice, and that the enemy should be deprived of it." General Hunter and other Union leaders therefore saw Georgetown and Winyah Bay as prime targets early in the war, and because the Confederates realized this, the area was well fortified and well garrisoned in anticipation of a full-scale invasion. A large-scale Federal invasion was never necessary, however. Within a few months of the fall of Hilton Head in November 1861, Confederate General John C. Pemberton, in overall command of what was then known as the First Military District of South Carolina (the area from the South Santee to Little River), ordered the area defenses stripped. As a result, many of the troops and twenty pieces of much-needed artillery were taken from the area forts and shipped to Charleston.

Colonel Arthur Middleton Manigault, the man Pemberton ordered to dismantle the forts and remove his troops from the district, predicted what would happen when the Federals learned that the area was undefended. He believed that "the destruction of the batteries and the removal of the troops would prove an invitation to the enemy too strong and too important to be resisted, the whole country lying at the mercy of a single gunboat." Manigault, who by that time was stationed far away from the coast (and who would later achieve the rank of brigadier general himself), was correct. He wrote:

> *The Federal Navy began to probe upriver…two U.S. gunboats entered the bay, and proceeded to Georgetown and up the neighboring rivers, and carried off many Negroes, destroyed much property, and created great alarm. These visits were repeated several times, and on the Santees like raids were undertaken by the enemy.*

After the Confederate batteries were dismantled, the Union navy took a much more aggressive approach along the upper coast of South Carolina. The incident to which Manigault referred occurred on May 21, 1862, when the USS *Albatross* and the USS *Norwich* entered Winyah Bay and, passing North Island, noted for the first time that the redoubt and lighthouse were deserted. The Federals could see that the forts on the bay were deserted, and so with no armament to stop them, the next day the

The USS *Albatross. U.S. Navy Historical Center illustration.*

As a lieutenant in the U.S. Army during the Mexican War, Arthur Middleton Manigault was wounded three times in five battles. Although he had been living as a civilian planter near Georgetown for over a decade before the Civil War, he was still regarded as a man of superb abilities and a natural-born soldier. He advanced from the rank of captain of his small unit of volunteers to the grade of brigadier general by the end of the war.

Albatross and the *Norwich* steamed into Georgetown. After a feeble attempt by the Confederates to turn the ships back—Confederate Major William P. Emanuel had his men set fire to the turpentine-laden brig *Joseph* and set it adrift—the Federals knew that they would henceforth have open access to the rivers that converged in the Georgetown area. That afternoon, the two Union ships went about ten miles up the Waccamaw River and raided a mill, carrying off eighty slaves in the process. As Commander George Prentiss of the *Albatross* noted, "The whole region around here could be taken possession of with little opposition."

While the Federals would never truly take "possession" until February 1865, for the next year they mounted an increasingly aggressive campaign of upriver fighting, which to some extent brought the economy in the area to a standstill. On June 5, Lieutenant I.B. Baxter, commanding the USS *Gem of the Sea*, took his ship into the South Santee River below Georgetown, where he picked up five "contrabands" (runaway slaves) from Blake's Plantation. This plantation had been abandoned by the owner shortly after the war began, when Blake, a native Englishman, returned to England after the fall of Fort Sumter. By 1862, the plantation was operating under the guidance of the overseer, John McGinnis, who would be killed at the plantation during the war when he was accidently shot one night by Confederate pickets. Slaves informed Lieutenant Baxter that although the plantation had more than six hundred slaves when the war began, nearly half had since died from illness and neglect.

Perhaps of more interest was that Baxter learned that Blake's Plantation was an outpost for Confederate troops guarding the Santee Rivers and that there were about three hundred Confederate cavalry stationed in the area. In the following days, Baxter visited South Island (there he noted that the abandoned Confederate fort was quickly "going to decay") and other sites at the mouths of the Santee Rivers, learning, among other things, that the steamer *Seabrook* and two schooners had recently run out of the South Santee, avoiding the Federal ships. The Federals started patrolling the area more carefully in light of this knowledge—capturing the runner *Louisa* and the tug *Treaty* on June 20—but even so it was obvious that in order to stop the blockade runners and have free access to the rivers themselves the area would have to be secured.

On June 24, a Federal expedition consisting of the *Albatross* and the steamers USS *Western World*, USS *E.B. Hale* and USS *Henry Andrew*, as well as the steam tug *North Santee* (the converted Confederate tug *Treaty*), headed into the mouth of the South Santee, and their primary mission was to try and steam about seventy miles upriver to destroy the Northeastern Railroad bridge. The Federals had failed to take into account the meandering nature of the rivers, as well as the draft of their ships, and both the *Andrew* and *Western World* were grounded almost immediately. By the time they actually began to make progress, it was June 25. As they proceeded, it became obvious that only one ship, the *E.B. Hale*, could actually make it upriver. Thus, the mission was aborted, and the ships headed back for the open sea.

By this time, the Confederates had amassed and were waiting for the Federal ships to come back. Confederate Major Stephen D. Byrd had learned of the ships' intentions the day before and had ordered Captain Christopher Gaillard's Santee Light Artillery and a company of cavalry under Captain Thomas Pinckney to garrison Blake's Plantation and lie in wait for the Federals' return. After discovering how many Federal ships were upriver, Byrd also sent a company of Captain Wheeler's infantry to their assistance.

The Federal ships were fired upon by "artillery, riflemen, and cavalry" as they came within sight of Blake's Plantation, and in return, Prentiss "shelled [the Confederates] into the woods." Prentiss then had the marines put ashore, forcing the Confederates into retreat. Lieutenant H.B. Lowry, in command of the marines, burned all of the buildings on the plantation, including the rice mill, and destroyed 100,000 bushels of rice. By that time, Byrd (who was now on-site himself) had formed up "my men into columns, dismounting 25 of Captain Pinckney's men, and plac[ing] them as skirmishers on the left of Captain Wheeler's company." Lowry's Federal marines came "at a double quick along the road…advanced and fired [on Byrd's] column." Both columns parried with one another, firing and firing again, until the Federals finally retreated to their gunboats. Behind the Confederate position, a smaller force of Federal skirmishers "made an attack on the rear" but were driven back by Confederate Lieutenant L. Bacot Allston and his men.

Neither the Federals nor the Confederates suffered many casualties, but one incident occurred that day that would have severe repercussions later. According to a report to Secretary of the Navy Gideon Welles from Rear Admiral Samuel DuPont, Commander Prentiss apparently "permitted the [plantation] to be plundered and a great many articles taken on board the steamers." While by 1865 plundering would fit into General Sherman's concept of total warfare, in 1862 it was still regarded as a barbaric practice—especially when one considered that the theatre of war was, after all, the United States. Prentiss then thought better of allowing his men to loot the plantation, and when the ships returned to Winyah Bay, he had his men surrender the goods they had stolen. One man, Assistant Paymaster Seymour F. Frizelle, apparently tried to conceal his ill-gotten gain, and his room was searched to reveal that he had been holding out. He was relieved of duty and sent north, and DuPont recommended his dismissal from the service.

After the failed raid, the Federals did have a victory of sorts to celebrate; they had acquired more than four hundred contrabands who had flocked to the protection of their gunboats, meaning that there were four hundred fewer slaves to work the Confederate plantations. These people were taken to North Island, where they could be cared for until arrangements were made

Early in the war, Rear Admiral Samuel Francis DuPont was considered one of America's leading naval officers, though his star would dim as the conflict raged on. *Civil War Photograph Collection, Library of Congress.*

to take them elsewhere. In one of those strange twists that come in times of war, one of the contrabands was a man named Robert Blake. In order to utilize the manpower available, the Federals asked the men on North Island for twenty volunteers to serve in the Union navy. Blake volunteered, and several months later, while serving on the USS *Marblehead* as a steward, his ship came under Confederate artillery fire while stationed in the Stono River. As Blake approached the *Marblehead*'s gun deck, he was knocked down by an explosion, and afterward, though a noncombatant, he began running powder boxes to Union sailors while under a heavy and consistent fire. For his bravery during the engagement, Blake was awarded the Congressional Medal of Honor on April 16, 1864; he was the second African American to be so honored and the first to actually receive the medal.

The Federals spent the last days of June and the first days of July probing, blockading and harassing. On June 30, Prentiss sailed into Georgetown and demanded that the wives of some citizens who were loyal to the Union be allowed to leave with him; this was readily agreed to. On that same day, Prentiss also had his ships ascend the Waccamaw River to secure five lighters of rice to feed the contrabands in his care, most of whom were the ones taken from Blake's Plantation. On July 1, Prentiss noted that the Federal ships seized "three lighters with 65 casks clean rice, and two lighters with rough rice," and on July 2 they captured the blockade runner *Volante*, loaded with salt and fish. With each captured blockade runner or raid on a plantation, it was clear that, with the Confederate forts dismantled, the only thing stopping the Federals from completely subjugating the people of Georgetown were the drafts of their ships. This, Prentiss knew, was a major impediment. By July 3, he declared attempts to get upriver a "failure" and noted that "the opinion is unanimous that we cannot get upriver, and I give it up." He ordered the *Hale* and the *Andrew* out of the area, and he left his station as well.

It was also clear that blockade runners such as the *Volante* were running the risk of frequenting the district because not only rice, but also salt, was still being produced and shipped out of the district. Earlier in June, Commander Prentiss had ordered a raid on the saltworks in Murrells Inlet, owned by planter John LaBruce and Captain Joshua John Ward of the Waccamaw Light Artillery. These works were making thirty or more bushels of salt a day, and although Prentiss's men landed and attempted to destroy the works, they were attacked and scattered by a force of about twenty-five

The Civil War from Georgetown to Little River

Confederate cavalry. While they had inflicted no damage on the works, in July they tried again. On July 21, the *Western World*, the *Gem of the Sea* and the *Treaty* steamed into Murrells Inlet and landed a party of raiders. While demolishing the salt-making apparatus, they were again attacked by about twenty-five Confederates. Though under fire, the Federals destroyed the saltworks, scattering the salt among the sand at a cost of only two Federal wounded. This successful operation set the tone for the destruction of the other saltworks along the Strand.

By this time, it was no secret that Pemberton had made a serious blunder by stripping the district of most of its artillery and men and dismantling the forts. Pemberton, however, an irascible man in the best of times, was not about to admit that he had made a mistake. After Adjutant and Inspector General Samuel Cooper suggested on July 5 that "it would be well to occupy…Georgetown, constructing the necessary works, and placing…a garrison of the best artillery sufficient to serve the requisite number of guns, so as to prevent the entrance of marauding vessels," Pemberton shot back, "We cannot protect the whole coast. If it is attempted to put guns in position at…Georgetown they will be lost." Cooper pressed, and Pemberton pressed back, saying on July 10, "It is absolutely impossible to put guns on…South or Cat Islands, near Georgetown. The enemy's gunboats can always prevent it; they command those places"—which, of course, they did because Pemberton had surrendered the positions by abandoning them without a fight.

On July 11, Pemberton again argued, "No more troops can be spared for the defense of Georgetown and vicinity. Heavy guns for that purpose are out of the question." Apparently now on the defensive himself, Pemberton went on to acknowledge what many others were in fact claiming:

> *There are persons who believe that the withdrawal of the batteries from Georgetown was a wanton exercise of power on my part, who assert that they were sufficient to have prevented the entrance of the enemy's fleets, and that I should even now be compelled to replace them. I am content to let these individuals enjoy their opinions, but I must, nevertheless, continue to act upon my own judgment unless controlled by superior authority.*

The Federals would use Pemberton's obstinate nature to their advantage. On July 29, Commander George Balch of the USS *Pocahontas* took his ship up the Waccamaw River, passing the abandoned earthworks at Laurel Hill Plantation along the way. There had been artillery pieces stored at Laurel Hill in 1861, and apparently the Waccamaw Light Artillery still used the earthworks, which Balch felt were well situated "on a high bluff," as a base of operations from time to time. Balch was worried that anchoring near the earthworks was risky because he heard that there were four pieces of artillery and a company of soldiers in the area and that there he "might…have my decks swept by the enemy…where I could do him but little harm." He moved his ships farther upriver, where they took on twenty-eight contrabands at Dr. Joseph Magill's plantation, site of Camp Magill during the early days of the war. Throughout his tour, all Balch found were abandoned earthworks and crumbling fortifications—a state of affairs that was about to change.

Fortunately for the citizens of the district, General Pemberton had at last been "controlled by superior authority" and was instructed to build new forts on Winyah Bay. On August 3, 1862, Pemberton visited Georgetown to select a site on which to build new forts to defend Georgetown and block access to the area rivers. Since the original forts on North, South and Cat Islands were now in Federal possession, Pemberton selected Mayrant's Bluff and Frazier's Point on Winyah Bay for the site of the new forts, and plans were made to strengthen the interior defenses along the major rivers while the large forts were being built, actions that would hopefully enable the planters to reach a level of productivity unseen since the Federals began patrolling the rivers.

Commander Balch, now the senior Federal naval officer in the district, was more concerned about events transpiring up the rivers at the time. He had received a report on August 7 that the Confederates had reoccupied the fort at Laurel Hill with a force of 150 men and that new earthworks up the Black River had been garrisoned as well. In addition, the Confederate steamer *Nina*, a ship that had been ferrying Confederate troops and supplies since the early days of the war, was operating freely on the inland rivers, and the Waccamaw Light Artillery seemed to be gaining strength and size and was operating without opposition. Once the battery at Mayrant's Bluff was built, the Federals would be effectively cut off from any further forays upriver, allowing the Confederates to carry on in whatever way they deemed necessary. Considering all of these factors, and after the uneventful trip up the Waccamaw River on the twenty-ninth, Balch determined that it was an opportune time for a raid up the Black River.

The Civil War from Georgetown to Little River

This page: Commander George Balch of the USS *Pocahontas* heard that 150 Confederates were stationed at these earthworks at Laurel Hill in August 1862. The view of the Waccamaw River from this bluff shows why Balch worried that if the four pieces of artillery and the company of soldiers reported to be there fired on him, he might have his "decks swept by the enemy...where I could do him but little harm." Today, the earthworks are in a remote part of the nine thousand acres encompassing Brookgreen Gardens and Huntington Beach State Park. *Photographs by the author.*

On August 14, Balch set out with the *Pocahontas* and the *Treaty* in search of the *Nina*, the Waccamaw Light Artillery and any fortifications that he could destroy. He had Lieutenant I.B. Baxter and a complement of men from the *Gem of the Sea* along on the *Treaty* for close-order work, and with this well-armed party, Balch began his ascent up the Black River. When they were about twenty-two miles upriver, the Federals came upon the first of the Confederate batteries at Sparkman's Plantation. Balch ordered his ship "secure with her broadside on the batteries at 500 yards distance. We then went to quarters and…delivered a broadside of shells and then opened with grape…at first gun the batteries were deserted and Ward's artillery went off in full retreat." When the batteries were abandoned, slaves flocked to the ship, and Balch ordered them taken onboard. The slaves told Balch that the Confederates had not really evacuated the area but were secretly massing in the woods and planning a counterattack. Soon, firing commenced from the woods, and Balch was beginning to realize the peril of his situation. His ships were hemmed in, and he was far from any reinforcements. The Confederates were peppering the decks of the ships with a steady fire. Reluctantly, Balch decided to abandon his search for the *Nina* and return to North Island. He ordered his ships to proceed upriver about three miles, where he turned his ships and passed the batteries again. This time,

> as we passed the earthworks we were fired upon by the enemy in ambush, distant only 50 yards…to which we replied with canister and grape from the great guns and howitzer and our riflemen with great effect…The bluffs were lined with troops, and for a distance of 20 miles we had to run the gauntlet, followed by the Treaty, which kept up a spirited fire from her howitzer and small arms.

Twice, the *Pocahontas* ran aground, but each time the *Treaty* towed it off. As the ships ran the gauntlet, "the bluffs afforded a chance for the enemy to fire down upon us, a good share of which the gallant little *Treaty* had to stand as she followed."

The Confederates, of course, had known that the ships were coming. Major William P. Emanuel and his men had deployed fieldpieces at Sparkman's Plantation and waited for the gunboats. They had only been in position a short time when the gunboats appeared, and Emanuel had his

The Civil War from Georgetown to Little River

Commander Balch's ship, the USS *Pocahontas*, was a screw steamer mounting six guns. This picture was taken at Edisto Island in 1861. *U.S. Navy Historical Center photograph.*

men open fire. From atop the steep riverbanks, the Confederates had the advantage of being able to fire down on the Federals, and after the Federals aborted their mission, Emanuel's men followed the ships downriver, firing from the riverbanks until the ships were at last out of range.

Once again, it had been a relatively bloodless affair. Although Emanuel claimed, "I don't think the enemy's loss could have been less than 50 killed and wounded," and his own casualties were just two wounded, Balch claimed his total casualties at one man critically wounded.

While it was clear to the Federals that there was no way to take and hold control of the area rivers, their frequent raids, the rice they were taking and the slaves they were harboring were causing economic chaos in the district. Those raids were about to become substantially more difficult, however. Confederate General P.G.T. Beauregard was given command of the district on August 29, 1862, and Pemberton was relieved of his position and transferred. Though no doubt a cause for celebration along the coast, the planters' good fortune would eventually bring about the misery of the whole Confederacy. Pemberton was given command of Vicksburg and was there vilified for surrendering that city in July 1863. After that, he was never again offered a command as a general officer, and he resigned his commission in 1864. He was eventually appointed a lieutenant colonel of artillery and served at that rank for the remainder of the war.

Beauregard was much more aware of the area's defensive shortcomings and the economic havoc that resulted, and he no doubt felt that he needed a man in charge of the district who knew the area and its importance. Beauregard named Georgetown native Brigadier General James Heyward Trapier as commander of the district, and Trapier set about refortifying the area that Pemberton had left defenseless. Though short of men and materials, within a few months Trapier had fortified Winyah Bay well enough to defend it from Union incursions. At the same time, batteries were being built along the Santee, and by November 10, Beauregard had also sent an engineer to examine the Santee to find sites for underwater obstructions, to fortify a battery at Nowell's Point and to construct a new battery on the North Santee at Ladson's Bluff.

Even though the batteries on the rivers and in Winyah Bay were in the early stages, Beauregard's refortification of the district would pay off sooner than expected. When on November 11 two Federal gunboats steamed into Winyah Bay and started firing on the fort at Mayrant's Bluff, soon to be known as Battery White, they were met by returning fire from the Second South Carolina Artillery under the command of Captain Frederick F. Warley. Captain Warley's men had by that time mounted nine pieces of artillery in the fort, and after a few minutes, the Federals retired. With the construction of the new batteries, the Federals were denied access to Winyah Bay and the rivers that emptied into it, and once again peace came to the plantations.

As General Manigault noted from afar, it was too late. Because most of the slaves were gone, many plantations lay in ruin, and the planters would never feel safe staying there again. Beauregard seemed to realize this as well, because by June 1863 he noted in a letter to Governor Milledge Bonham that a battery planned up the Santee at Taber's Point would not be armed or manned, as all available armament and artillerists had been sent to Georgetown. He consoled Bonham with the thought that there were six guns at Lenud's Ferry manned by Gaillard's Light Artillery, but otherwise the lower Santee was undefended. It was obvious that even if the Federals were once again denied access to some sections of the area rivers, the Union navy had essentially accomplished its objective of denying the area's rice supply to the Confederacy.

The Civil War from Georgetown to Little River

Having effectively curtailed much of the rice being produced in the area, the Union navy next turned its attention to shutting down the remaining salt production in the district. The Federals had not been sitting idly by in the first years of the war, of course. On November 24, 1862, the USS *Monticello* had bombarded and destroyed two extensive saltworks near Little River Inlet. This, coupled with the destruction of the Murrells Inlet saltworks in July, left only the largest saltworks in the district, Vaught's saltworks on Singleton's Swash in what is now Myrtle Beach, still functioning. Vaught's saltworks consisted of some thirty buildings in four separate works and a 100,000-gallon cistern, as well as an inventory of two to three thousand bushels of salt on hand at any one time. The owner, Peter Vaught, had been so alarmed by the July 25 attack by the Federals on the LaBruce and Ward saltworks that, on August 8, he had written to Columbia and asked the state for troops to guard his property. Though at the time General Pemberton had been unable to spare any troops for the works, on October 31 the South Carolina Executive Council saw to it that state troops, Captain Ed Boykin's Wateree Mounted Riflemen, were temporarily sent to Vaught.

By 1864, Winyah Bay, the Santees and Little River were fairly well blockaded. Rather than take a chance on losing men and ships in high-risk operations, the Federals seemed to have a sense that the war was winding down, and thus military operations in the area at that point generally consisted of raids that deprived the Confederacy of much-needed supplies. On April 20, Commander A.K. Hughes of the USS *Cimarron* received reports that the Confederates would be removing as much as fifteen thousand bushels of rice from a mill five miles up the Santee, and that night Hughes ordered a party of thirty armed men to land near the mill. The next morning, his men raided the mill to find only five thousand remaining bushels, which they summarily destroyed.

This raid would almost pale in comparison to the damage inflicted by the USS *Ethan Allen* that same day and the next. Early on the morning of the twenty-first, the *Ethan Allen* set out from Murrells Inlet and headed northward up the coast. Having heard from escaped slaves about the immense saltworks owned by Peter Vaught, Master I.A. Pennell of the *Ethan Allen* had determined to find the works and destroy them. While heading up the coast, the *Ethan Allen* was hailed from time to time by people on the shore, and in each instance it sent out a boat and picked up a few contrabands seeking freedom. Other than the occasional party of people wishing to surrender, the trip up the coast was rather uneventful, as expected.

By about 2:00 p.m., the Federals were offshore of the saltworks, and Pennell and Ensign William Mero took twelve men and headed for the beach. As Pennell's boats approached the shore, those onboard saw about thirty men run into the woods. After landing, Pennell's men saw three other men sitting on a nearby fence, and these men immediately surrendered. As Pennell noted, he then deployed his "men as pickets to prevent a surprise, Mr. Mero taking the rest as a working party to destroy the works. On examination we found the works much more extensive than I expected."

The works were extensive, even more so than when Vaught had first requested and received troops for garrison duty in 1862. Since that time, one of the three warehouses on the property had been converted to a blockhouse, "with loopholes on all sides," not unlike Fort Randall. In addition, Pennell noted that there were enough lumber and materials for extending the works to double its size. This would have been no small feat, since the works already mounted forty-eight salt pans, with twelve more standing ready to be mounted.

Pennell's men quickly set about the business at hand. "After breaking all the pans and making it impossible to repair them, and having no other way of destroying the salt, I had it mixed with sand…then set fire to the buildings," Pennell noted. As the fire consumed the buildings, Pennell and his men took their prisoners and some escaped slaves who had joined them and headed for the ship. In less than three hours, Pennell and his men had destroyed the largest saltworks between Georgetown and Little River. And they weren't finished yet.

By nine o'clock the next morning, the Federals were off of Withers Swash, where they encountered yet another person on the shore waving a white flag. Mero took out a boat, picked up the man and brought him back to the ship. The man, a North Carolinian named Allen Jones, claimed to be a commissary sergeant in the Confederate army. He told Pennell that yet another saltworks could be found at the swash, complete with a furnace and boilers. Pennell sent out two boats under Executive Officer W.H. Winslow and Ensign James Bunting, whose men expediently destroyed the works and were back on the ship by eleven o'clock. That being done, Pennell took the *Ethan Allen* back down the coast; he and his men arrived safely in Murrells Inlet by four o'clock that afternoon.

The Civil War from Georgetown to Little River

Pennell's expedition had destroyed the last operable saltworks along the coast from Georgetown to Little River. With the rice plantations ceasing to operate except on a very limited basis, the salt industry had been the area's last fully functioning industry, and the destruction of the two works at Murrells Inlet, several around Little River and those at Singleton's and Withers Swashes had left the district without a major industry with which to boost its economy. In addition, with the Vaught works and blockhouse destroyed, the Confederates now had no base of operations on the coast between the North Carolina line and Waccamaw Neck. Although by that point, with the saltworks destroyed, there was now little of value on the coast for the Confederates to protect, this still left a large gap in the district's makeup and in essence forced all of General Trapier's troops into a small pocket of resistance around Georgetown. Ultimately, however, it did not matter. Both rice and salt production had basically ceased, and by February 1865, the Federals would completely control the coast from one end to the other. By April 1865, the war would be over, and neither the rice nor the salt-making industries would ever recover.

THE PLANTATION BATTERIES AND SALTWORKS TODAY

As the rice fields and many of the plantations fell into ruin after the war, so did the batteries that once protected them. Many of the plantation homes still exist today, though the plantations no longer produce rice; nor do they have saltworks. The ravages of wind and weather have now all but obliterated most traces of many of plantation batteries as well. As for the Confederate camps, it isn't clear exactly where any of these outposts were. While there are general indications in Confederate records about the locations of some camps in the district, the exact locations of camps such as Camp Magill, Camp Waccamaw, Camp Trapier, Camp Chestnut, Camp Harlee and Camp Middleton will probably never be known.

To some degree, the same is true of the area's saltworks, though salt making had long been a significant industry in the area even before the war. The saltworks that are mentioned in Civil War reports existed as early as 1825, when they were included in *Mill's Atlas*. More specific locations for the saltworks generally exist, even if the saltworks themselves do not. According to an article by C.B. Berry on the "Myrtle Beach Salt Industry,"

This page and next: A number of very clearly defined earthworks exist today on Wachesaw Plantation. According to the sign, they were built in 1863, and the fort was never used. *Photographs by the author.*

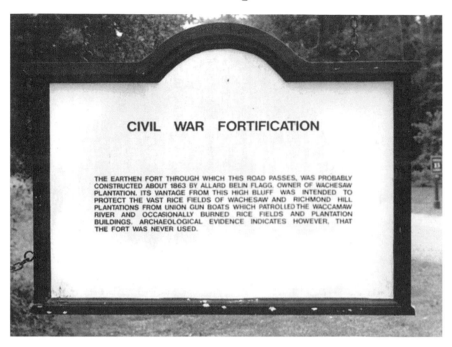

CIVIL WAR FORTIFICATION

THE EARTHEN FORT THROUGH WHICH THIS ROAD PASSES, WAS PROBABLY CONSTRUCTED ABOUT 1863 BY ALLARD BELIN FLAGG, OWNER OF WACHESAW PLANTATION. ITS VANTAGE FROM THIS HIGH BLUFF WAS INTENDED TO PROTECT THE VAST RICE FIELDS OF WACHESAW AND RICHMOND HILL PLANTATIONS FROM UNION GUN BOATS WHICH PATROLLED THE WACCAMAW RIVER AND OCCASIONALLY BURNED RICE FIELDS AND PLANTATION BUILDINGS. ARCHAEOLOGICAL EVIDENCE INDICATES HOWEVER, THAT THE FORT WAS NEVER USED.

golfers at the Dunes Club in Myrtle Beach "often drive their balls across a small round tidewater lagoon on Fairway No. 11" that may have been the site of Peter Vaught's "large salt water storage tank." Berry goes on to note that "nearby, along the banks of Singleton's Swash marsh, one can still see outcroppings of old brickwork which might have been the foundation and furnaces for the cast iron salt evaporating pans." No doubt there are other ruins along the Strand that pass for the crumbling foundations of old houses but are, in fact, related to the many saltworks that once existed there. However, none can be identified with any certainty.

As for the plantation batteries, there are still fairly extensive earthworks at Laurel Hill in a restricted-access area. Wachesaw Plantation is also the site of a rather large fortification. Though other earthworks may exist along the rivers, most have now been lost to the ravages of time, wind and weather.

CHAPTER FOUR

"He Was Hung Immediately after Capture"

The Assault on Murrells Inlet

Early in the war, when the initial Confederate defense perimeter was set up along the coast from Georgetown to the North Carolina line, Murrells Inlet was seen as an area of some value, but it was not, of course, regarded as being nearly as important as Georgetown or even Little River. While Georgetown had the deep-water access of Winyah Bay and was the feeder point for five major rivers, and Little River had a moderately sized port and was the northernmost anchorage on the South Carolina coast, Murrells Inlet had none of these attributes. The inlet was too close to Georgetown to be a viable alternative to that port, and the inlet had no inland river outlets. What the inlet did have was a series of twisting and turning channels that ran through numerous marsh islands, oyster beds and mud banks, and any cargo shipped into the inlet had to be unloaded and moved inland. As the conflict waged on, however, and both Georgetown and Little River were blockaded and effectively bottled up, Murrells Inlet, almost as an afterthought, became the focus of attention for the Union navy. The inlet was frequently visited by blockade runners, and furthermore, as the Federals tried to land patrols to attack targets in the inlet, they were met with defeat after defeat. By 1863, Murrells Inlet—sometimes referred to as "Murray's Inlet" in Federal correspondence—had become a prime target for the Federals along the northern South Carolina coast.

One reason that the Union navy was much more aggressive mid-war toward Murrells Inlet rather than Georgetown and Little River was because, while Little River was guarded by Fort Randall and Georgetown was defended by Battery White, by 1863, Murrells Inlet had no fortifications or artillery. Early in the war, when the first forts had been built at Little River, and at North, South and Cat Islands near Georgetown, Murrells Inlet had been fortified as well. Named Fort Ward in honor of planter Joshua John Ward, the earthworks there contained three guns and were initially manned by soldiers from Smith's battalion, which later became the Twenty-sixth South Carolina Regiment. A letter from Major William Capers White dated April 13, 1861, noted that he had deployed "twenty six men and two officers" of the Waccamaw Light Artillery to Murrells Inlet and "twenty men and two officers" of the Wachesaw Riflemen to the redoubt at Murrells Inlet. The ubiquitous Waccamaw Light Artillery was, in fact, the most far-ranging Confederate unit along the coast during the war, having been stationed variously from Little River to the South Santee.

Fort Ward was built when the district was under the direct command of General Robert E. Lee, who favored strong lines of coastal and interior river defense. Lee was transferred to Virginia in March 1862, and the man who succeeded him in command of the district, General John C. Pemberton, almost immediately made the unpopular and costly decision to dismantle almost every coastal fort north of the Charleston area and concentrate on defending that port instead. At that time, the largest regiment of infantry in the district (the Tenth South Carolina Regiment), most of the cavalry, all of the guns and ordnance stores and, in essence, everything of military value were removed. With the exception of the Waccamaw Light Artillery and a couple of companies of the state troops that would later become part of the Fourth and Seventh South Carolina Cavalry, the district was almost undefended by mid-April 1862. Fort Ward was decommissioned and stripped of its artillery as well, and the troops were left with only the humble quarters of a nearby Confederate camp named Camp Waccamaw.

It didn't take long for the Federals to begin probing actions in the area after they realized that the fortifications were abandoned, though most of the Federal incursions were naturally in and around Winyah Bay and Georgetown. During this period, the most active Federal ship in the area was the USS *Albatross*, commanded by George A. Prentiss, who repeatedly led his ships and others into the area rivers and destroyed anything of value to the Confederates. In June, Murrells Inlet saw its first direct action when Prentiss ordered a raid on the saltworks there. The saltworks in question were owned by planters John LaBruce and Captain Ward, and these works were capable of producing thirty to forty bushels of salt a day, making them a tempting target for the Federal raiders. However, when Prentiss's men landed and attempted to destroy the works, they were attacked and scattered by a force of about twenty-five Confederate cavalry. Unable to do any damage to the works, the Union troops were forced to return to their ships.

The saltworks were the object of a much more successful raid on July 21, when Lieutenant I.B. Baxter of the USS *Gem of the Sea* led a force to finish the job of destroying the saltworks in Murrells Inlet. Baxter took the *Gem of the Sea*, along with the USS *Western World* and the USS *Treaty*, into Murrells Inlet and landed a party of raiders. While demolishing the salt-making apparatus, they were attacked by a force of about twenty-five Confederates. The Confederates opened fire from the woods, but Baxter's men drove their attackers off at a cost of only two Federal wounded. The Union sailors finished the work of destroying the saltworks, scattering the salt in the sand before returning to Winyah Bay. This was the first occasion on which saltworks were destroyed in the district, setting the tone for similar attacks that would eventually occur at Singleton's Swash, Withers Swash and Little River. It was also the first significant action in the environs of Murrells Inlet, but during the coming year, Murrells Inlet would see as much action as any place along the northern coast of the state.

The Confederate high command realized the enormity of the mistake Pemberton had made in stripping the area of its defenses, and Battery White was built at Mayrant's Bluff on Winyah Bay. The firepower at this position kept Union ships out of the bay, and so for most of 1863 and almost all of 1864, the Federal navy contented itself with simply blockading Georgetown. Murrells Inlet began to see increased attention because, with Georgetown blockaded, runners had to find nearby ports to debark their goods, and Murrells Inlet was the only option within sixty miles. Since the Union navy didn't have enough ships in the area to effectively blockade Georgetown, Little River and Murrells Inlet, Murrells Inlet was left relatively uncovered. As it became clear that blockade runners were using Murrells Inlet as a safe haven, the Union navy was forced to take action.

In April 1863, the Union navy seemed to finally realize that Murrells Inlet was seeing a great deal of shipping traffic, and as such, it was a viable threat to the sanctity of the blockade. Lieutenant Commander D.L. Braine of the USS *Monticello*, which was stationed in Little River, noted that for

John Clifford Pemberton's rise through the ranks was enigmatic; by October 1862, he was a lieutenant general. After being vilified for surrendering Vicksburg in 1863, he resigned his commission and served the remainder of the war as a lieutenant colonel of artillery. General Pemberton's brief tenure as commander of the Department of South Carolina, Georgia and Florida was likewise marked by controversy. *Civil War Photograph Collection, Library of Congress.*

almost four hours he gave chase to a blockade runner heading south from Little River that ultimately got away. In doing so, he noticed that in Murrells Inlet "there are five large schooners and large buildings, evidently storehouses." Braine noted that this corroborated information that he had received from prisoners he had taken off of the blockade runner *Sue*, and he wrote to his superior, Captain Charles S. Boggs, "With your permission, I can easily destroy them in a day, and I would like to do so, if it meets with your approval." Boggs did approve and confirmed that the USS *Matthew Vassar* had also noted several ships in Murrells Inlet. He instructed Braine to "make a careful reconnaissance of the inlet after the moon goes down" and said that he would send down the USS *Chocura* and the USS *Violet*, as well as launches with twelve-pound howitzers. "With these," Boggs said, "I hope you can clear out this nest...if successful, run no risk in bringing out prizes, but destroy them."

At sunrise on April 27, 1863, the USS *Monticello* and the USS *Matthew Vassar* appeared at the inlet and began shelling the ships at anchor there. The Federal ships bombarded the inlet for about two hours, and the Confederate cavalry stationed there under the command of Major William P. Emanuel, without artillery to return the Federal fire, was at the mercy of the Union artillerists. Major Emanuel quickly sent word to Lieutenant Colonel Joseph Yates in Georgetown (General Trapier had been temporarily reassigned to Sullivan's Island) to send up some rifled artillery and additional troops as quickly as possible. When the shelling stopped, the Federals sent out three boats under the command of Acting Master L.A. Brown. These boats contained forty-seven men and five officers who had but one purpose: destroy as many ships and as much property in Murrells Inlet as quickly as possible.

After landing, the Federals fanned out and crossed a sand spit, where they came upon a shallow marsh. They waded across the marsh and came upon the schooner *Golden Liner*, which the men, under Lieutenant Braine of the *Monticello*, subsequently burned, along with two storehouses nearby. Before them was a wealth of plunder, all theirs for the taking. Along the wharves of the inlet were another two schooners, a sloop and, best of all, more than two thousand bales of cotton waiting to be loaded. But before they were able to dispense with the riches in front of them, they were warned by a slave that there was a force of two hundred Confederate infantry and cavalry on the way, and the thunder of hooves alerted them

This 1861 drawing from *Harper's Weekly* shows the USS *Monticello* shelling Confederate troops at Fort Hatteras in North Carolina, much as the *Monticello* and USS *Matthew Vassar* would do in Murrells Inlet in April 1863. *U.S. Navy Historical Center illustration.*

to the approach of Major Emanuel and Company E of the Fourth South Carolina Cavalry. Rather than risk an encounter with a force reportedly much larger than their own, the Federals returned to their ships. Although one Federal sailor was wounded and another was captured in the retreat, all of the others made it back to the Union ships safely. At that time, the *Monticello* and the *Matthew Vassar* resumed their bombardment of the inlet, action that continued until the ships withdrew later that afternoon.

The Confederates had been lucky, for Lieutenant Colonel Yates had been unable to send the reinforcements in time, and only sheer bravado born of desperation had enabled Emanuel's cavalry to drive off the Federals. Yates knew that such a tactic was unlikely to work again, and it was apparent that he would have to reinforce the inlet by weakening the other sectors of his command. This decision was based on the fact that Murrells Inlet was receiving anywhere from five to seven blockade runners a week, more than any port along the northern South Carolina coast. Yates immediately called up a section of artillery from Georgetown, as well as requesting that Captain Boykin bring down his mounted riflemen stationed at Fort Randall. Still, Yates knew that if the Federals committed all of their resources, these reinforcements would not be enough. "They are not aware of present force at that point," he wrote of Murrells Inlet on April 29, "and will no doubt make another effort [to attack]."

If Yates had known about Braine's reports to his superiors, he would have indeed been worried. Braine's brief and only marginally successful raid had completely changed the Federals' perception of Murrells Inlet. His report noted that Murrells Inlet was the "grand depot of cotton… averaging five to seven vessels a week, [that] the cargo out is exclusively cotton, and they have never met with any interruption in their trade until today. Vessels are now expected here daily, with large supplies of clothing and stores of every kind." He added, "I think it is important that this point should be closely watched."

The Union navy didn't wait long to act on Braine's information. On May 3, the USS *Maratanza* and the USS *Chocura* anchored off of Murrells Inlet and began shelling in a preamble for another attack. The bombardment continued until 11:00 a.m., when the Federals sent ashore a small boat filled with seven men under the command of Ensign J.C. Gibney, apparently intent on burning some of the four schooners now anchored in the inlet. Although Captain Boykin's riflemen had returned to Little River, Major Emanuel's men of the Fourth South Carolina Cavalry were still at the ready. Having guessed what was coming after the experience of the Federal bombardment and attack the previous week, Emanuel had taken great pains to conceal his men in the hope of surprising the Federals and thereby capturing them without precipitating a full-scale firefight. Some of the Confederates showed themselves prematurely, however, and a skirmish quickly erupted. Owing to the strategic placement of his men, Emanuel's cavalrymen killed one Federal sailor and seriously wounded three others while suffering no casualties themselves. The remainder of the landing party was driven back into its boats while the *Maratanza* and *Chocura* provided covering fire, and so, for the second time in a week, the Federals had to beat a hasty retreat.

Although the Federals did capture the blockade runner *Success* off the inlet later that day, it was a hollow victory considering that their prime target had been the ships in the inlet. There was no hiding the fact that, once again, operations in Murrells Inlet had been a Union failure, and in light of this, Commander G.H. Scott of the *Maratanza* was more cautious in his assessment of the inlet than Braine had been. Scott was *convinced from the rebel forces at this place of the utter impracticability of attempting a boat expedition for the destruction of the vessels, as the route is long, circuitous, and protected for a great distance by thickly wooded banks, affording the best possible cover for the large number of infantry now collected here.*

What the Federals did not know, however, was that only a few days later the district was subjected to another diminution of Confederate troops, this time resulting in the removal of the companies of the Fourth South Carolina Cavalry that had defended Murrells Inlet so ably while stationed at Camp Waccamaw. Colonel Yates pleaded with the high command to let him keep Emanuel's men, claiming that otherwise he would have only enough men to man Battery White in Georgetown. He was allowed to keep Emanuel's troops until their replacements—two companies of the Twenty-first Battalion Georgia Cavalry—arrived on May 8. In addition to the Georgia troops, in Murrells Inlet and Georgetown, Yates had a company of cavalry under Captain John H. Tucker, Captain Ward's Waccamaw Light Artillery and Company D of the Second South Carolina Artillery under Lieutenant William E. Charles. Although the Georgia troops would be retained after Emanuel's cavalry left on May 9, Yates was told that holding Murrells Inlet was not a high priority, as it was "not regarded as of great military importance."

Apparently, the Federals felt otherwise, and on May 8, Rear Admiral Samuel DuPont actually ordered additional ships "to go into Murrells Inlet," including the USS *Conemaugh* and the USS *Flambeau*, and instructed the *Flambeau*'s captain to "establish a blockade off that entrance." On May 11, the *Conemaugh* and the *Monticello* anchored about two thousand yards off of the inlet and began shelling, and it appeared that when the Federals landed their troops, as they always did when the artillery barrage ceased, Murrells Inlet would most surely be sacrificed. Yates's troops were so thinly spread at that time that any Federal attack would have easily forced the Confederates to surrender or flee. But once again, luck was with the Confederates.

The captain of the *Conemaugh*, Commander Reed Werden, reported that "the inlet was too narrow for [his ship] to enter," and he had also been informed that in the last week "the enemy have increased their force,

The Civil War from Georgetown to Little River

The USS *Conemaugh* was a nine-gun side-wheel steamer with a crew of 125. Despite the fact that the ship was too large to enter Murrells Inlet, it was nevertheless able to shell the inlet and seriously damage a number of Confederate runners at anchor there. *U.S. Navy Historical Center photograph.*

having now artillery, cavalry, and infantry." Because of this, and because the five blockade runners at anchor in Murrells Inlet were unable to maneuver due to a precariously low tide, the Federals instead took aim at the ships, which gave them some very inviting targets. Werden estimated that in two and a half hours his ship alone fired more than one hundred rounds of ammunition, and the Federal bombardment damaged all of the ships. One, the *Golden Liner*, was completely destroyed. The *Golden Liner* had been disabled since the attack of April 27, and this time it was finished off. In addition to the damage suffered by the ships, the shelling set fire to and destroyed one hundred bales of cotton that had been on the wharves ready to be loaded. Despite the damage to the ships, the Confederates had gained some time, and they remained in possession of the inlet.

While trying to decide what to do about Murrells Inlet, the Federals did assign the *Flambeau* to full-time blockading duty there. This was a departure from their previous strategy, which had been simply to have blockaders from Georgetown and Little River try to monitor the inlet with overlapping patrols, a strategy that clearly had not worked. After the *Flambeau* was stationed there, traffic to the inlet seemed to slow, and the occasional capture of a blockade runner, such as in the case of the seizure of the *Bettie Cratzer* off of Murrells Inlet on June 23, was about the only activity of note during the summer that followed, other than the fact that in June General Trapier had grudgingly returned to retake command of the district. Trapier knew that his station in Charleston was more important, and so to him, returning to the Georgetown area must have seemed tantamount to a demotion.

Perhaps the most significant event that occurred that summer was that Rear Admiral John A. Dahlgren took over command of the South Atlantic Blockading Squadron, and he took a much more aggressive approach to completely shutting down all ports on the South Carolina coast. In a letter dated October 16 to Master W.L. Babcock of the USS *T.A. Ward*, he ordered Babcock to Murrells Inlet "for the purpose of observing a strict blockade of the place." He also warned Babcock to "take every precaution in communicating with the shore in search of wood or water." Despite the warning, Babcock and the *T.A. Ward* were soon to be involved in the first of a series of embarrassing incidents in Murrells Inlet that would incur Federal censure from as far away as Washington, D.C.

It began inauspiciously enough on October 17, when the blockade runner *Rover* attempted to run into Murrells Inlet and, failing to do so, was driven ashore. From that point on, the Union and Confederate accounts often differ substantially. According to the Confederates, the *Rover*'s crew removed some of its cargo to a spot behind the sand dunes and then "the vessel was burned by the crew." The Federals claimed that two boats sent out from the *T.A. Ward*, under the command of Ensign Myron Tillson, arrived on the ship to find one man onboard and the ship "loaded with a full cargo of cotton." The ship was fast aground, and there was no way to move it; therefore, Master W.L. Babcock of the *Ward* later wrote, "Mr. Tillson set fire to and destroyed her." The *Ward* fired three rounds into the ship to keep anyone from attempting to put out the fire, as well as pumping three shells "into the [nearby] Rebel barracks" for good measure.

Had events ceased at this point, it would have been a simple enough affair, but on the twentieth things began to get complicated. A party from the *Ward* led by Ensign Tillson, in a boat with a twelve-pound howitzer, headed into shore "for the purpose of shelling a large frame building, where it [was] supposed Rebel cavalry were concealed." They shelled the building for about thirty minutes, and then Babcock sent in another boat in command of Master's Mate A. Elwell, who was to "assist the first cutter in effecting a landing" to find water. Tillson took eleven men with him to reconnoiter and left seven others behind in the boat in the charge of Elwell. Tillson's men saw a schooner, the *Cecilia*, up in the inlet and decided to investigate to see if it "could be cut out or destroyed." They walked over the dunes and right into Company B of the Twenty-first Georgia Cavalry under Lieutenant Ely Kennedy.

Ensign Tillson and his men had stumbled into the area where the *Rover's* cargo was concealed, and Confederate Brigadier General James Trapier would later claim that he believed they were actually looking for that cargo, not the *Cecilia*. Lieutenant Kennedy's men had been watching the Union sailors since they landed, and Trapier reported that Kennedy had "concealed a portion of his men, dismounted," and "another body (mounted) was ordered to make a dash upon the enemy's rear as soon as fire was opened upon them in the front, and cut off their retreat." The Federals were taken completely by surprise. Lieutenant Kennedy's men killed one of Tillson's men and captured the others, even though the Confederates faced a covering fire from both the barges and the *T.A. Ward*. The other seven Federals retreated to the barges, but Trapier reported that "several men were seen to fall when the retreating barges were fired upon." The Confederates apparently suffered no casualties. The Federal prisoners were sent on to Columbia and ultimately to Andersonville, where no doubt some paid the price of the failed mission with their lives.

General Trapier reported the incident to his superior, P.G.T. Beauregard, who wrote in reply on October 25, "Officers and men on outpost service, by coolness, vigilance, subordination, and resolution, may frequently render signal service by successful small encounters with the enemy." The reaction on the Union side, after yet another failure, was not so congratulatory. On November 4, Dahlgren wrote to Secretary of the Navy Gideon Welles regarding the capture of Tillson and his men and noted that the Confederates were using the inlet because the "perfect blockade of Charleston is driving speculators to the smaller ports." "I shall dispatch a gunboat to stop that game," Dahlgren wrote, and indeed by the sixth he noted that he had sent the gunboat USS *Ottawa* to Murrells Inlet. Welles, however, was not so easily appeased. He blamed the impromptu actions of officers who seemed to be looking for glory for events such as the *Ward's* fiasco and no doubt remembered that, just a few months earlier at Little River, an almost identical event had led to the capture of eight men from the USS *Matthew Vassar*. Welles wrote that the Department of the Navy "must express its disapprobation of officers and men straying from their vessels, either with or without permission, resulting in their capture. Stringent measures are needed to correct this evil, and a general order should be issued by the commanding officer of each squadron forbidding it." If Welles was incensed by the *T.A. Ward* incident, his anger would pale in comparison to what must have been his reaction to the affair of the USS *Perry* in December of that year and would lead to one of the most controversial events to take place along the South Carolina coast during the war.

On December 5, 1863, Ensign George Anderson from the brig USS *Perry* landed two boats and twenty-two men just below Murrells Inlet. Their mission was to set fire to the *Cecilia* and destroy any Confederate outposts they discovered. Furthermore, if they encountered any trouble, they were to signal the *Perry*, which would cover their retreat with its guns. It should have been a relatively simple operation: find the ship and destroy it, or if there was trouble, signal the ship and retreat. As Dahlgren said later, however, "It was a blundering affair, without judgment on the part of the commanding officer, and aggravated by the alleged disobedience of the officer sent ashore in charge of the party."

Ensign Anderson's first concern was that right before he was sent ashore he was given "verbal orders" from Acting Master Samuel Gregory, commander of the *Perry*, to take along George Brimsmaid, a black freedman, and "send him ahead, unarmed, as a scout"—an order that Anderson apparently found puzzling. Once they landed on the beach, Anderson posted Sam Gregory Jr.—the captain's son—as signalman on a dune, telling him to signal the ship at the first sign of trouble. Anderson and the rest of his men then started for the *Cecilia*.

Almost immediately things started to go wrong. Anderson noted that Sam Gregory Jr. came running toward them, "crying out that the enemy's cavalry were approaching," but Anderson was incensed that Gregory had abandoned his post and that he hadn't signaled the *Perry* to extract or cover the party. Anderson grabbed the flag and tried to signal, but the Confederate cavalry—Captain H.K. Harrison and a company of the Twenty-first Georgia—bore down on them and forced their retreat. They had nowhere to go; another company of cavalry under Captain C.C. Bowen came bearing down on the boats. Finding his men cut off and trapped in a crossfire, Anderson looked to the *Perry* for help. Inexplicably, though, the *Perry* "was lying head-on to the beach so that her guns could not be brought to bear." Anderson and his men were trapped, and with five wounded, he surrendered his command.

As Anderson and his men surrendered, one of his seriously wounded men, John Pinkham, was injured so badly that he couldn't rise from the ground; nevertheless, he was ordered to get up "by one of the rebel captains." When he failed to do so, "the captain shot him with his revolver," giving him a mortal wound. Then, when Anderson and his men were taken to the Confederate camp, two cavalrymen took the freedman Brimsmaid off into the woods. Anderson reported that they saw one of the Confederates strike him in the head with a saber as they left camp, and moments later, they heard a yell and two gunshots. The two Confederates returned alone, claiming to have hanged Brimsmaid, and Anderson said that the Confederate officers later confirmed this.

For whatever reason, Captain Gregory waited more than a week before sending in a party under a flag of truce to inquire about his men. On December 15, he sent a party in to ask "if any of the men were killed, and if so how many; also, who were wounded; also if any were uninjured." The Confederate officer with whom he talked at first "declined to answer the questions," but Gregory eventually discovered that his son was uninjured and that the prisoners would be treated well. Apparently satisfied, Gregory let it go at that. Ensign Anderson and his men were shipped off to Confederate prisons, and the final Federal toll was four dead (including Brimsmaid and one man who died in Andersonville), and one sailor who had to have his leg amputated due to wounds. Although the Confederates themselves suffered one man killed and another two wounded, it was yet another failure in Murrells Inlet for the Union navy.

There was a great deal of controversy about whether Brimsmaid was actually murdered. Predictably, Confederate records mention nothing about this event, and in fact, the only possible reference is an oblique one on December 8, when General Trapier mentioned that a "missing prisoner is not yet officially accounted for." Admiral Dahlgren himself wasn't sure that there was anything to it. In January 1864, long before the captured Anderson's report would be filed in October, Dahlgren noted that "as regards the murder of one of the *Perry*'s boat crew, it seems to be derived from some contrabands who escaped subsequently from the inlet."

"On examination I do not learn that any one of the party witnessed the murder, or saw the man, or had seen any person who had done so," Dahlgren wrote to Welles. Gregory also claimed that he couldn't substantiate the rumor, writing, "I have no evidence that he was hung. All that I have heard in regard to him was a rumor, coming from the USS *Nipsic*, that he was hung immediately after capture."

Whether or not the murder occurred was no more important than the fact that many Union seamen believed it had occurred, and this, coupled with yet another Federal failure in Murrells Inlet, made many Union naval officials very, very angry—and they couldn't seem to distribute the blame fast enough. Dahlgren blamed Gregory and Anderson entirely for the mission's failure, and Gregory may have used the fact that Anderson was wasting away in a Confederate prison camp to shift a portion of the blame to his subordinate. Dahlgren claimed that he was "not satisfied with the account given by Acting Master Gregory" and removed him from command of the *Perry* shortly thereafter. The admiral was also tired of dealing in small measures with Murrells Inlet, which had become a major annoyance:

> *I desire…to administer some corrective to the small parties of rebels who infest that vicinity, and shall detail for that purpose the* Nipsic, Sanford, Geranium, *and* Daffodil, *and also the sailing bark* [Ethan] Allen *and the schooner* Mangham, *100 Marines for landing, and four howitzers, two for boats, two on field carriages, with such boats as may be needed.*

Dahlgren planned a full-scale invasion of the inlet and attended to every detail of how the landing should go. "Throw up a slight breastwork of sand across the spit, and post a field piece behind it," he wrote. "Pits for riflemen can also be made…Let the howitzers use grape and canister mostly." Because of Pinkham's and (allegedly) Brimsmaid's murders by the Confederates, Dahlgren was also very careful to make sure that his men did not take out their frustrations on the local populace and cautioned them to "allow no injury to be done to defenseless women and children or to their habitations and necessaries of life." He did not address what they should do in the case of captured Confederate soldiers.

On December 29, 1863, the USS *Nipsic*, USS *Sanford*, USS *Daffodil* and the USS *Ethan Allen*, with a landing force of 250 men, set out for Murrells Inlet, and on the thirtieth they were joined by the USS *George Mangham*.

The Civil War from Georgetown to Little River

The ships were poised for a dawn attack that would hopefully atone for the frequent humiliation that the Union navy had suffered since focusing its attention on Murrells Inlet some months earlier. But again, it was not to be. As dawn approached, a storm front moved in and dispersed the ships waiting to attack. Fate, it seemed, had again thrown in on the side of the Confederates and the attack was subsequently canceled.

On January 1, the *Nipsic* returned to bombard the inlet and to destroy a schooner it had spotted there earlier, but there would be no amateurish bravado or half measures on this occasion. Dahlgren noted that with workmanlike precision, two launches with forty men escorted in two cutters with thirty marines, who were "deployed as skirmishers across the spit, while a launch with a howitzer took position to enfilade any advance on their front by the Rebel cavalry." They opened fire on the schooner, and at "the fifth round she took fire and, with a valuable cargo of turpentine, was soon in one blaze." These men returned to the *Nipsic* without mishap and without seeing the "four companies of soldiers, principally cavalry" that they expected to confront there. Dahlgren wrote, "I trust this correction will serve to moderate any gratification which the rebels may have derived from the capture of our boat's crew."

It is doubtful that Dahlgren really felt that burning one ship had evened the score. For all their efforts, the Federals had faced a frustrating year in Murrells Inlet, their only accomplishments of note being the capture and destruction of a few blockade runners. In May 1864, Dahlgren wrote that he and General John Porter Hatch, who had more than fourteen thousand men in his command, had been planning "an incursion…into the country between Georgetown and Murrells Inlet," but Hatch was assigned other duties and the plans were cancelled. Thereafter, the Union navy was content merely to blockade the port instead of wasting troops trying to raid the ships that slipped in. With Little River and Murrells Inlet blockaded, the navy once again turned its attention to Georgetown, and as the Union navy focused on Georgetown, so, too, did the Confederates shift their troops there, away from the now useless anchorage at Murrells Inlet. After all of the wasted Union effort trying to subdue the tiny port of Murrells Inlet, the Confederate high command ultimately did the job for them: further cutbacks in troops for the district eventually saw the port relinquished to the Federals without a fight.

General John Porter Hatch was in command of the Department of the South in 1864, and he and Admiral Dahlgren formulated a plan to invade "the country between Georgetown and Murrells Inlet" by deploying some of Hatch's fourteen thousand troops. *Civil War Photograph Collection, Library of Congress.*

This *Mill's Atlas* map of 1825 shows the location of several saltworks in the Murrells Inlet area, as well as some of the twisting, shallow waterways that the Federal navy found so frustrating. *Library of Congress Map Collection.*

The Civil War from Georgetown to Little River

MURRELLS INLET TODAY

Murrells Inlet has the odd distinction of being the area that physically looks most like it did during the Civil War, but it is also the only section of the coast where there are no visible remains from the conflict. Fort Ward's location has always been a mystery, but given that it was probably on the oceanfront in an area that has altered greatly over the last 150 years, there seems to be no trace of the small three-gun battery. There are two inland batteries near Murrells Inlet, which were addressed in an earlier chapter, but on the oceanfront itself no trace of a redoubt remains. As for the shifting channels, mud banks and sand spits, they are just as tricky and ever changing as the frustrated Union navy found them to be in 1863.

CHAPTER FIVE

BLOCKADERS AND
BLOCKADE RUNNERS

Civil War enthusiasts who visit the South Carolina coast looking for historical landmarks turn to places and things such as cannons, earthworks and even the plantations that dot the landscape, and all provide tangible evidence of the war. However, one largely forgotten facet of the war along the Grand Strand is one for which the only physical evidence remaining are the rotting timbers of burned-out hulks that now rest on the bottom of the Atlantic or far beneath the sands of the shores of the barrier islands. The blockade runners destroyed along the Strand during the war provided the backdrop for a number of exciting encounters that occurred there, often with far more frequency than the land-based actions detailed elsewhere in this volume.

The Confederate fortifications built in 1861 served the district well during those periods when they were well garrisoned and armed. There was no sustained Confederate naval presence in the area, other than the CSS *Nina*, a 400-ton side-wheel steamer armed with one gun, and the *Treaty*, a small steam tug. Neither of these ships were really used for offensive naval maneuvers and instead served as transport and reconnaissance vessels. Federal reports from 1862 note that the *Nina* came "down daily from the direction of Georgetown, keeping within the shoal water, and generally" stayed inside the bay below North Island, then "looking around, immediately return[ed]." Consequently, while the *Nina* and *Treaty* were not well-armed gunboats, both were viewed as more than a simple nuisance, and the destruction or capture of both would become Federal priorities later in the war.

The Federal navy, on the other hand, had a considerable presence as the war progressed, though initially few Union ships were stationed in the area. This was probably owing to a failure to recognize exactly how important the area was economically, as well as a failure to realize that not only Winyah Bay but also Little River and Murrells Inlet were safe havens for blockade runners. In 1861 and 1862, however, lacking the troops, ships and armament to occupy and hold the sixty miles of coastline between Georgetown and Little River, the Union navy instead contented itself with an occasional foray up the area rivers or the shelling of a fortification. The Federals did have enough ships on station most of the time to at least patrol the coast, and because the South needed its ships to have the ability to move in and out of the area to transport goods and supplies, a cat-and-mouse game between the blockaders of the North and the blockade runners serving the South took place throughout the war. While it was generally a one-sided affair to the advantage of the Union navy, the crafty blockade runners kept the Federals on the move until the last months of the war.

After the war began in 1861, several events occurred that indicated that neither the North nor the South had quite settled into the conventional drudgery of the blockade as it would come to be once both sides were acclimated to the idea that they were at war for the long haul. Because of the economic importance of the area due to its rice production, many in the state felt that a Union invasion would surely come. As a result, when in August 1861 there was a report of Union troops landing near Pawleys Island, it was taken quite seriously. Colonel Arthur Middleton Manigault, commander of the Confederate forces in Georgetown, took the *Nina*, loaded with two companies of infantry and the Georgetown Artillery under Captain James G. Henning, and proceeded up to Hagley Plantation on the Waccamaw River. The Union landing turned out to be a false alarm, but the Confederate response indicates that the Confederates knew the area was vulnerable to seaborne invasion and that they would treat every threat as a very real possibility.

For the most part, however, 1861 was a relatively uneventful time in terms of blockading and blockade running, and indeed, much of the naval action involved wrecked Union ships captured by Confederate troops stationed on the shore. On August 9, a Union steamer sank after being wrecked by a storm off of Georgetown, and the crew of nineteen was captured and placed in the Georgetown jail. That same day, Colonel Manigault took a detachment of men onboard the *Nina* and captured another Union ship disabled during the storm. On November 2, the steamer *Osceola*, commanded by Captain J.T. Morrill, foundered off of Georgetown, and two boats of crewmen were taken captive and sent to North Island and then on to Charleston.

The first significant combative encounter involving a blockade runner occurred on December 24, 1861, when the blockade runner *Prince of Wales* grounded while attempting to run in at North Inlet just above North Island. At about seven o'clock that morning, Union Lieutenant Irvin Baxter of the *Gem of the Sea* saw the *Wales* running close to the shore and started firing on it. The third shot damaged the Confederate ship, and after four more shots, the captain of the *Wales* had apparently had enough and ran it into North Inlet. Just inside the bar, however, the ship was grounded, and as the *Gem of the Sea* neared the beached runner, the runner's captain put the *Prince of Wales* to the torch before abandoning it. Baxter had Union seamen put out in boats, and after boarding the *Wales*, they attempted to put out the fire and attach a hawser from the runner to the *Gem of the Sea* to tow it off.

As they started towing the *Wales*, a company of Confederate cavalry led by Captain John H. Tucker opened fire on the Federals from the north shore of North Inlet, and while under a heavy fire, the ship ran aground once again. Baxter's men tried to tow off the ship yet again, but by that point they were also receiving fire from a separate Confederate patrol led by Lieutenant R.Z. Harllee from Company D of the Tenth South Carolina Regiment. Lieutenant Harllee had posted his men behind the sand dunes and ordered them to open fire, and Baxter later wrote, "The bullets fell over and around…as fast as the scoundrels could fire their pieces." The Federals eventually gave up trying to tow off the ship and returned to the *Gem of the Sea*; they were "greeted with terrific yells from the rebels on [North] island, and also with another charge of musketry." Both sides watched the ship burn to the waterline—the Federals out a prize and the Confederates out a cargo of fruit and salt.

Soon thereafter, Colonel Manigault was informed that one thousand to fifteen hundred Union troops had landed on North Island, and though this proved to be a rumor, the next day a Union transport ship loaded with troops passed so close to North Island that the soldiers onboard could clearly be seen by the Confederates. On February 14, 1862, the *Gem of the Sea* sighted a schooner trying to run in at Georgetown, and after firing on it and chasing it for three hours, the schooner escaped. On February 27, the *Gem* once again saw a schooner believed to be the *British Queen* trying to run into Georgetown, and though the *Gem* lost it in the darkness that night, it was captured in Wilmington by the USS *Mount Vernon* the next day. On March 12, the *Gem of the Sea* sighted the British blockade runner *Fair Play* off of Georgetown, but this time the chase would not be in vain. The Federals stopped and boarded the side-wheel steamer, which was carrying a cargo of fish, soap, candles and a variety of materials that most likely would have been used for Confederate uniforms. After its capture, the *Fair Play* was armed with four twelve-pound howitzers and converted to a Federal ship of war later that year.

On March 29, the USS *Keystone State*, with William Le Roy commanding, was stationed in Georgetown, and almost immediately upon its arrival, Le Roy learned that the Confederate steamer CSS *Nashville* had been in Georgetown from the twentieth until the twenty-seventh. Although the *Keystone State* had missed the *Nashville*, Le Roy would have known the *Nashville* by reputation, as it had been the first ship to fly the Confederate flag in England when it arrived in Southampton in October 1861.

The Confederate steamer CSS *Nashville* would be a constant irritant to the Federal navy. It was the first ship to fly the Confederate flag in England when it arrived in Southampton in October 1861, and until its destruction in Georgia in February 1863, it was a highly sought-after prize. *U.S. Navy Historical Center illustration.*

The Civil War from Georgetown to Little River

On April 3, Le Roy did not miss his quarry. The *Keystone State* chased the runner *Seabrook* as it was coming out from Georgetown. The *Seabrook* ran back into the Santee, where Le Roy reported that it bottomed and was crippled, although apparently the Confederates saved the ship because it would be seen running the blockade just a month later, on May 19. On April 10, Le Roy spotted the 180-ton schooner *Liverpool* trying to run into Georgetown, and as the *Keystone State* chased it, it, too, grounded. This time, the destruction was complete as its own crew burned it to prevent its capture.

Le Roy had a more tangible prize on April 15 when the *Keystone State* captured the blockade runner *Success*. Along with the *Gem of the Sea*, the *Keystone State* chased a suspicious ship for about two miles before overhauling it. Though the ship flew a British flag, Le Roy learned that it was "the former privateer *Dixie*, lately the *Kate Hale*, and now the *Success*." Le Roy noted that despite any claims of neutrality, the captain of the *Success*, D.L. Benton, had been a lieutenant on the *Dixie*, and that ship "had obtained quite a reputation during her piratical cruise." Le Roy seized the ship, its crew and the cargo of "100 bales of cotton, 234 barrels spirits turpentine, 40 bushels peanuts, and 3000 pounds rice."

It was evident that the Santee Rivers, Winyah Bay, North Inlet and even Murrells Inlet and Little River had become ports of call for a number of blockade runners that were visiting the area with increasing frequency, as had been demonstrated by the frequent encounters in which the *Keystone*

The USS *Keystone State. U.S. Navy Historical Center illustratioin.*

State had engaged during just over two weeks on station. Le Roy wrote to Union Admiral Samuel F. DuPont on April 25, 1862:

> *I would respectfully call the attention of the flag officer to the importance of Georgetown as a place for receiving and distributing supplies for the rebel States, and of the necessity for more vessels to blockade its waters, there being several outlets, extending some 10 or more miles, that render the blockade by sailing vessels very inefficient, and even with the most extreme vigilance one steamer is incapable of properly blockading.*

The Federals would indeed assign more steamers to the area, but not because Le Roy suggested it; rather, they did so because Confederates gave them an opportunity that could not be passed up. On May 21, 1862, the USS *Albatross*, commanded by George A. Prentiss, and the steamer USS *Norwich*, commanded by Lieutenant J.M. Duncan, entered Winyah Bay and learned that the Confederate forts that had previously kept them out of the bay, as well as the rivers, had all been abandoned. Though the Federals saw some Confederate cavalry, they encountered no other opposition. Therefore, on May 22, the *Albatross* and the *Norwich* steamed into Georgetown, "within 30 yards of the houses," and though the Confederates set fire to the brig *Joseph* and set it adrift in a feeble attempt to block the Federal ships, it was clear that the Union navy now had free access to the area. Later that afternoon, the two Union ships went about ten miles up the Waccamaw River and raided a mill, and on May 26, the Federals proceeded upriver again. Because the Confederates had been expecting such a move, this time the ubiquitous state cavalry commanded by Captain John H. Tucker exchanged gunfire with the Federal ships, forcing them to withdraw. These river forays did not come without a price to the few Federal ships in the area, however, and blockade runners were taking advantage of the Federal ships being out of position. On that same day, the runner *Lucy Holmes* ran out of the South Santee with a cargo of rice, and not long afterward, the runners *Emma* and *Caroline* ran out as well.

On June 3, the *Gem of the Sea* captured the blockade runner *Mary Stewart*, and on June 20, the *Albatross* captured the schooner *Louisa* on the Santee River loaded with 147 bales of cotton and two lighters of rice. Perhaps the biggest prize that day came when the Federals' old nemesis, the tug *Treaty*, was captured off the Georgetown bar. The *Treaty* proved to be a great prize. It was renamed the *North Santee*, sheathed with two-inch planks, armed with a rifled howitzer and turned against the troops it had formerly served. On June 24, an expedition consisting of the USS *Albatross*, the USS *Western World*, the USS *E.B. Hale*, the USS *Henry Andrew* and the *North Santee* set out upriver to destroy the Northeastern Railroad bridge. Because of low water, several of the Union ships were grounded again and again. Ultimately, the mission was scrapped, and the Federal ships headed back for the sea. Back downriver, Confederate troops were lying in wait, and after a skirmish at Blake's Plantation, the Federal ships returned to their posts off the bar—though with four hundred slaves they had liberated during the raid. These contrabands were sent to North Island, and though it was often rumored that the Confederates were planning to massacre them—Baxter of the *Gem of the Sea* noted that there were about "500 troops at Georgetown, consisting of cavalry, infantry, and artillery, who intend crossing over in boats from Georgetown to [Pawleys] Island and from thence to the north end of North Island, with the intention of destroying the contrabands"—the intended raid would never amount to more than a rumor.

On July 2, the USS *Western World* captured the British runner *Volante* in Winyah Bay, and though the Federals were still catching blockade runners, it was also obvious that a number of Confederate ships and runners were sitting upriver, out of harm's way. Baxter noted that the Confederate ships in the area, both military and runners, consisted of the *Nina*; the *Weenee*, a 50-ton side-wheel steamer; the *Orah Peck*, a 150-ton schooner; and the *General Ripley*, a 175-ton side-wheel steamer. The *Nina* was of course the same *Nina* that had been a nuisance since the war began, and the Federals finally decided that the ship needed to be captured or destroyed. Therefore, on August 14, the *North Santee* (or *Treaty*, as it was once again being called by the Federals) and the USS *Pocahontas* set out from Georgetown to "capture the steamer *Nina* up the Black River." Armed at that time with one ten-inch gun and four thirty-two-pounders, the guns of the *Pocahontas* would have been more than a match for the single gun of the *Nina*.

When they were about twenty-two miles upriver, the Federals came up against Confederate batteries at Sparkman's Plantation. The Federals returned fire with "a broadside of shells and…grape," but then, suddenly, the Confederates also began firing on them from the woods. As the Confederates maintained a steady fire on the Federal ships, Commander Balch decided to abandon his search for the *Nina* and return to North Island.

He noted that all the way back to Winyah Bay, his ships were kept under a constant fire from Confederate troops along the riverbanks, and the "gallant little *Treaty*" took the brunt of the fire as it followed the *Pocahontas*. Although the *Pocahontas* ran aground twice, the *Treaty* towed it off, and the Federals returned to Winyah Bay having failed to locate and destroy the *Nina*. As they would soon learn, the *Nina* had already been taken out of action for them, and its boiler and other "machinery had been removed…rendering her as a possession useless to us." It would serve the Confederacy no more.

Not all blockade runners headed for the safety of Georgetown, of course; Little River and Murrells Inlet sheltered runners as well. However, due to the narrow mouth of Little River and the twisting, shallow waterways at Murrells Inlet, once blockade runners were known to be harbored there, it was easier to bottle them up there than it was in Winyah Bay. It was also easier to land raiding parties there in a position to cut across the beaches and destroy ships at anchor. On June 25, 1862, Union boats from the USS *Penobscot*, the USS *Mystic*, the USS *Mount Vernon*, the USS *Victoria* and the USS *Monticello* went to the town of Little River and destroyed two schooners, sixty bales of cotton, two hundred barrels of turpentine and fifty-three barrels of rosin. On November 2, 1862, the USS *Penobscot* captured the runner *Pathfinder* off of Little River. Federal blockaders captured the schooner *Florida* as it attempted to run out of Little River on January 11, 1863, although this successful capture was followed by several misses in February. The USS *Matthew Vassar* let a runner trying to enter Little River Inlet slip away on the twentieth, and on February 22, the *Vassar* and the USS *Victoria* reported missing both a steamer running out and a runner trying to come into the inlet.

An exciting encounter took place on the night of February 24, 1863, when a steamer, camouflaged for the night run by being painted completely black and having no masts, tried to run into Little River and encountered a patrol boat from the *Matthew Vassar*. The steamer hailed the *Vassar*'s boat, and the Federals told the runner that they were Confederates. The runner, which was undoubtedly the British steamer *Hero*, was notified that it was being boarded. Sensing a trap, the captain of the runner decided to run, and the Federals in the boat fired rifles and small arms, ordering the *Hero* to stop. Despite the fact that the *Matthew Vassar* came up and fired a broadside at the *Hero*, the runner escaped. Later that same night, at Little River, the British schooner *Annie* was captured by the USS *State of Georgia*.

The Civil War from Georgetown to Little River

On March 21, the USS *Victoria* fired several shots at a large side-wheel steamer trying to run in and captured the *Nicolai I*, an English ship loaded with dry goods, arms and ammunition. On March 30, the USS *Monticello* captured the steamer *Sue* off of Little River. The *Sue* was considered "an old offender, having run the blockade before," and had recently unloaded salt somewhere between Georgetown and Little River.

Farther south, a relatively rare event occurred on January 15, 1863, when a Union supply ship was wrecked on North Island. The *Lotus*, a ship out of Boston carrying supplies for the Federal troops stationed at Port Royal, ran ashore, and though the Federals on the USS *Sebago* tried to tow it off, after moving it about twelve feet, a storm surge pushed it even farther up the beach. The Federals decided that removing the ship was impracticable and began removing its cargo. Commander Beaumont of the *Sebago* noted that when his men were removing the cargo, they were surprised to find among the sutler's store and barrels of potatoes "casks of liquor…put up in various ways for smuggling." The Federals removed some of the cargo, though much had been lost when the ship beached.

On February 24, the English blockade runner *Queen of the Wave*, which Federal reports later called a "new and magnificent vessel," ran aground in the North Santee River, and it was set on fire by its captain to keep it from being captured, even though its hold was full of valuable goods, including morphine, opium and quinine. But on the morning of the twenty-fifth, the ship was still visible, and it was obvious that the fire had never reached the intensity needed to burn the ship and the blaze had gone out. Lieutenant Commander T.H. Eastman of the USS *Conemaugh* immediately sent out boats to destroy the ship, lest the Confederates begin salvage operations and recover the ship's cargo. But as the *Conemaugh*'s men boarded the *Queen*, they discovered onboard seven Confederate soldiers of the Waccamaw Light Artillery who had been conducting salvage operations all night. Unable to escape, the Confederates, led by Lieutenant Philip R. Lachicotte, were forced to surrender and were taken aboard the Federal ship USS *Quaker City* and ultimately sent to a Northern prison. Eastman's men completed the destruction of the ship by blowing up the *Queen of the Wave*.

As events in January and February had shown, conflicts between the blockaders and the runners were increasing, and 1863 would see large-scale action up and down the Strand. On April 27, the USS *Monticello* and the USS *Matthew Vassar* began shelling Murrells Inlet and, two hours later, landed more than fifty men to destroy as many ships and as much property in Murrells Inlet as they could. They first burned the schooner *Golden Liner* and then two houses, but as they turned to destroy another two schooners, a sloop and over two thousand bales of cotton, Confederate cavalry chased them back to their ships.

The Federals began to pay greater attention to Murrells Inlet, however, after reports that the traffic there was "most brisk…averaging five to seven vessels a week." On May 4, the *Monticello* and the USS *Chocura* began shelling the inlet in a preamble for another attack. After the bombardment, the Federals again sent ashore soldiers to burn some of the ships anchored in the inlet, but again, the Confederates repulsed them, this time killing one Federal soldier and seriously wounding three others. The remainder of the landing party was driven back into their boats, and for the second time in a week, a Federal landing party just barely escaped. Again, on May 12, the *Conemaugh* and the *Monticello* anchored about two thousand yards off of the inlet and began shelling. Although there were five blockade runners at anchor in the inlet and none of them was able to maneuver due to a precariously low tide, the Federals could not maneuver or move into the inlet either. The Federals still claimed a victory of sorts in that the bombardment had damaged all of the ships, and one, the *Golden Liner*, which had been disabled since the attack of April 27, was completely destroyed.

The Federals would rarely leave Murrells Inlet so uncovered after events of the spring, and naturally, fewer runners tried to run in as the Federal presence increased; in fact, that summer the capture of the blockade runner *Bettie Cratzer* on June 23 was the only activity of note. In October, the fifty-ton blockade runner *Rover*, loaded with cotton, attempted to run into Murrells Inlet on the seventeenth, and, failing to do so, the schooner was driven ashore. Its crew removed its cargo to a spot behind the sand dunes and then put the ship to the torch. Two days later, boats were sent out from the USS *T.A. Ward* under Ensign Myron Tillson to destroy the cargo and the damaged schooner *Cecilia*, which was a mile and a half away. The *Ward*'s men were thwarted by Confederates from the Twenty-first Georgia Cavalry under Lieutenant Ely Kennedy, and Kennedy's men killed one of Tillson's men and captured several others, even though the Confederates faced a covering fire from both the barges and the *T.A. Ward*. Most of the prisoners eventually ended up in the infamous Confederate prison at Andersonville.

After the capture of the *Margaret and Jessie*, it was commissioned as the Federal warship USS *Gettysburg* in 1864. *U.S. Navy Historical Center illustration.*

On November 5, the Federals captured the *Margaret and Jessie* off of what is now Myrtle Beach. The capture of this particular ship had become somewhat of a priority with the Union navy, as it had successfully run the blockade at least fifteen times. So determined were the Federals to capture the runner that when she was sighted off Wilmington, no fewer than four Federal ships—the transport USS *Fulton* and the USS *Nansemond*, the USS *Howquah* and the USS *Keystone State*—were sent after it. When it was finally overtaken, it was quite a coup for the Federals. Later that month, on the fourteenth, the schooner *George Chisolm* was captured running out of Georgetown with a cargo of salt. It was overtaken near the South Santee by the USS *Dai Ching*, under the command of Lieutenant Commander James C. Chaplain.

On December 5, a crew of thirteen men and three officers under the command of Ensign William B. Arrants from the brig USS *Perry* landed on what is now Litchfield Beach. These men were to work their way up to Murrells Inlet to destroy a schooner at anchor and ready to run out that night. But as soon as the Federals hit the beach, they were met by Captain H.K. Harrison and a company of the Twenty-first Georgia Cavalry. Both sides exchanged fire, resulting in two Federals being seriously wounded before the party surrendered to the Confederates, who themselves suffered one man killed and another two wounded. Although one of the Federal enlisted men escaped, the Confederates had once again been successful in thwarting a Federal attempt at mayhem in Murrells Inlet.

In order to shut down Murrells Inlet, which was clearly becoming a major haven for blockade runners, on December 29, the USS *Nipsic*, the USS *Sanford*, the USS *Geranium*, the USS *Daffodil* and the USS *Ethan Allen* began a concentrated bombardment of Murrells Inlet to disperse any Confederates stationed there. Federal artillery sporadically softened up the area until December 31, when the five Union ships were joined by the USS *George Mangham*—complete with a landing force of 250 marines. The ships were poised for a dawn attack, but a storm front moved in and dispersed the ships. After yet another failed attempt to shut down Murrells Inlet, the Union navy would not again attempt a full-scale invasion in the district until February 1865, preferring instead to remain on station and blockading the inlet so that the runners would look elsewhere.

Georgetown, however, could not simply be blockaded and let rest, and as 1864 began, there were several encounters with blockade runners seeking to enter Winyah Bay. The first of these involved the runner *Dare*, which had left Bermuda in early January and, upon attempting to enter Wilmington, had been chased off. It was pursued by the Federals until it was finally run aground twelve miles north of Georgetown at North Inlet on January 7. Rather than risk having the Federals tow it off, the captain of the runner evacuated the passengers and crew and set fire to the ship. Shortly thereafter, boats from the USS *Aries* and the USS *Montgomery* attempted to land a shore party of four officers and twenty-four sailors to put out the fire and salvage the ship, but halfway to shore, the barges capsized in the rough seas and three of the Union seamen drowned.

As the survivors from the barges made their way to shore, they found a party of three men—Major William P. White, commander of the Twenty-first Georgia Cavalry, and Second Lieutenant Thomas Young and Private Lemuel Robertson, both of Company C of White's regiment. Major White noted that he and his men, with no support and without firing a shot, "gallantly charged upon 25 Abolitionists…[and] armed with cutlasses and pistols…compell[ed] them to lay down their arms when there was no supporting forces within three quarters of a mile of the parties." White explained that "to my surprise, instead of one volley at least, the whole party, commanded by a lieutenant of the U.S. Navy, obeyed the summons, were taken prisoners." Perhaps the rough seas had taken the fight out of the Federals, but it was yet another bitter experience for the Federal navy. Just a few days later, however, on January 12, the *Aries* would have more luck when it left the blockade runner *Vesta* "a complete wreck, with five feet of water in her" at Little River.

On March 1, the USS *Connecticut* came upon the blockade runner *Scotia*, a side-wheel steamer out of Glasgow, and gave chase. The *Scotia* had left Wilmington the previous evening loaded with 220 bales of cotton, but

Men from both the USS *Montgomery* (top) and the USS *Aries* (bottom) attempted to capture the *Dare*, but their boats were overturned in the rough seas. The survivors were captured by Major William P. White and two men of the Twenty-first Georgia Cavalry. *U.S. Navy Historical Center illustrations.*

after just a two-hour pursuit, the *Connecticut* had its prize. By April 15, the Federals had stationed two more ships, the USS *Ethan Allen* and the USS *Cimarron*, in the Georgetown area, and within days these ships had made an impact on the Confederates in the district. On April 21, the *Cimarron* slipped up the Santee River and destroyed a rice mill and the five thousand bushels of rice stored there, though this would almost pale in comparison to the damage inflicted by the USS *Ethan Allen* that same day and the next. Early on the morning of the twenty-first, the *Ethan Allen* set out from Murrells Inlet and headed northward up the coast, having heard from escaped slaves about the immense saltworks on Long Bay owned by Peter Vaught. The works were extensive and included three warehouses, one of which was a Confederate blockhouse. In addition, the works mounted forty-eight salt pans, with twelve more standing ready to be mounted. Pennell's men set about "breaking all the pans…destroying the salt [by mixing it] with sand…then set[ting] fire to the buildings." At nine o'clock the next morning, they destroyed another saltworks at Withers Swash and arrived safely in Murrells Inlet by four o'clock that afternoon.

On June 2, 1864, a Union sentry in the North Island Lighthouse spotted a ship lying close offshore near North Inlet at about nine o'clock that morning, and Master Charles W. Lee thereafter. The ship was the side-wheel steamer *Rose*, and the *Wamsutta* apparently chased it away from Winyah Bay. Owing to the low tide, the *Wamsutta* was unable to look for the ship any further until three o'clock, but surprisingly, the *Rose* was still in the area. As soon as the *Rose* saw the *Wamsutta* approaching, it ran for the south end of Pawleys Island. Lee reported that it then "ran ashore near the wreck of another steamer and some buildings on the beach; the whole crew, consisting of about 20 persons, making their escape over the bows and by their boats, hastened by a rifle shell thrown at them by our 20-pounder Parrot." The *Wamsutta* "threw a few shells and stands of grape into the buildings and woods and bushes, to clear them of any skulkers," and then Lee sent Ensign E.R. Warren and Second Assistant Engineer Henry Wanklin with a boat's crew and specific orders to try and save the vessel if possible. Hardly had the Federals boarded it when a force of about seventy-five Confederate cavalrymen came from the direction of the north end of the island. Lee's men attempted to attach a rope from the *Rose* to the *Wamsutta* and tow it off, but the runner was firmly mired in the sand and would not budge. By this time, Lee noted, "the cavalry had advanced to the edge of the woods, and commenced firing at our men on board the steamer, who returned their fire, and I also shelled the woods, which kept them back."

By then it was nearly 7:00 p.m., and the Federals, finding it impossible to tow off the ship, decided to destroy its engines and then set it afire, eliminating the possibility that the Confederates might find something usable among the ashes. The only cargo that the Federals discovered onboard were "some barrels and cases of liquor and small stores," but Lee was certain that the ship had been unloading during the afternoon as it sat at North Inlet. The *Wamsutta* remained offshore until the wreck was consumed by fire, and then it returned to its station near North Island. On June 9, Lee headed back to check the wreck and found "a large party of mounted men near the wreck and buildings, at which I fired several shells, stands of grape, and round shot." The bombardment drove away the Confederates, who "had apparently been at work trying to save the iron and parts of the machinery of the wreck of the *Rose*."

The destruction of the *Rose* was not significant in itself, for most of the cargo had ended up in Confederate hands as intended. But unbeknownst to the forces in the area at the time, the *Rose* would become perhaps the last blockade runner destroyed near Georgetown. After that, few Confederate ships would be successful trying to enter Winyah Bay because, as was the case in most Confederate ports in late 1864, the Union navy was now well in control of the surrounding waters. In fact, from that time on, the Federals would take a much more aggressive offensive approach, and in October 1864, they began planning to mount an expedition to destroy the Confederate navy yard up the Pee Dee River at Mars Bluff, as well as the impressive Confederate gunboat being built there, the CSS *Pee Dee*. Ironically, one of the factors in the construction of the *Pee Dee* was that it, too, was to some degree dependant on the blockade runners trying to bring supplies into the district. A letter dated December 1864 from Edward J. Means, commander of the Mars Bluff navy yard, instructed his paymaster to proceed to Georgetown to remove supplies "now on board the steamer *Carolina*" and return them to Mars Bluff. Clearly, the *Pee Dee* was in the final stages of its completion and would become a formidable obstacle if it descended into Winyah Bay.

Rear Admiral John Dahlgren sent the USS *Pawnee* to Georgetown to take on the *Pee Dee*, and at 221 feet long and 47 feet wide, with a 10-foot draft, the *Pawnee* was a formidable adversary. The crew of 181 manned an impressive array of firepower—two twelve-pounders, eight nine-inch smoothbores, one one-hundred-pound Parrot rifle, four nine-inch Dahlgren smoothbores and two other smaller guns—giving the ship by far the most firepower of any Federal ship in the district. As another chapter in this work details, the battle between the two ships would never take place. Just as the Confederates had decommissioned the *Nina* earlier in the war, at about the same time that the Federals had committed themselves to destroying it, so, too, they decommissioned the *Pee Dee*. Boxed in on the Pee Dee River, the Confederates destroyed the *Pee Dee* to prevent its capture.

At the other end of the coast, on February 5, 1865, Little River saw its final action as the war wound to a close. Federal commander William B. Cushing, who had led a daring mission that resulted in the brief capture of Fort Randall at Little River in January 1863, took fifty men in four boats from the USS *Monticello* and went up to subdue or demand the surrender of the town of Little River. The few Confederates there readily surrendered, and Cushing's men destroyed an estimated $15,000 worth of cotton that was sitting on the wharves ready to be shipped out. Cushing noted that the citizens "professed to be willing to come back under the old government, and most of them seemed to be loyal men, only awaiting the emancipation from military rule." In Little River, the war was over.

After the fall of Charleston on February 17, 1865, all major Southern ports were controlled by Federal forces. Georgetown was one of the last large ports in Confederate hands—and it, too, would soon fall. On February 25, Georgetown surrendered and was occupied by a force of Federal marines from the USS *Catalpa* and USS *Mingoe*, but not before the last vestiges of Confederate cavalrymen in the area dashed into town and skirmished with the Federals for fifteen minutes before withdrawing. Admiral John Dahlgren proclaimed martial law in Georgetown on February 26, and with the guns of the *Mingoe* trained on the town and the marines in place, for the first time in four years Georgetown was under the flag of the United States of America. By that time, the Federals had amassed a large flotilla in Winyah Bay, and during the last two weeks of February and up until the first of March, the USS *Mingoe*, the USS *Catalpa*, the USS *Harvest Moon*, the USS *Chenango*, the USS *Clover*, the USS *Flambeau*, the USS *Geranium*, the USS *Mcdonough*, the USS *Nipsic*, the USS *Pawnee*, the USS *Sonoma* and the USS *Sweetbriar* were all stationed in and around Georgetown. Some of these ships explored the area's rivers, some stayed outside of the bar and some just waited so that they would be on hand if any Confederate retaliation occurred.

The Civil War from Georgetown to Little River

With the destruction of the CSS *Pee Dee* in early March, the Federals had no obstacles to prevent them from having free access to the waterways, and by March 6, Union gunboats cruised the area rivers, carrying the message of freedom and emancipation to the thousands of slaves roaming the district. Although there was no longer any organized Confederate opposition in Georgetown, there were small pockets of resistance along the rivers and farther inland. On March 7, the USS *Chenango* was fired on by Confederate cavalrymen patrolling about forty-five miles up the Black River. The cavalrymen took position behind a levee and began to pour a rapid rifle fire upon the Federals. The commander of the *Chenango*, Lieutenant Commander George U. Morris, ordered his ship about and fired a broadside at the levee with the *Chenango*'s guns. The Confederates quickly dispersed, and Morris took his ship back downriver.

Surprisingly, the Union navy found itself viewed as a welcomed protector rather than as a vile invader as the war came to a close. In March 1865, some of Georgetown's leading citizens even met with Captain H.S. Stellwagen aboard the *Pawnee*, hoping that since he commanded the Federal navy in Georgetown he might be able to help control the growing number of lawless slaves in the area. By mid-March, the problem had become worse. In addition to the former slaves who were causing trouble, bands of renegade Confederate deserters now roamed the district. The abandoned plantations along the waterways offered ample shelter to the lawless vagrants, and whenever they wanted something, they usually took it from the defenseless citizens living in the area. As the war was not over, most of the able-bodied men of the district were away, leaving as easy prey the women and children who made up the majority of the population at the time. Eventually, the Federals posted troops in Conway, hoping to keep the raiders from any further incursions. This did, in fact, help keep the deserters out of the town, but by then they were roaming the waterways as well. A gang of about thirty deserters were said to have commandeered a flatboat and were raiding up and down the Waccamaw River. Captain Stellwagen ordered the *Mingoe* upriver to search for the marauders. Later in the March, another expedition was mounted to drive out the deserters, this time involving the *Mingoe*, the *Catalpa*, four large launches, ten boats and three hundred troops. In addition to clearing out the raiders, Stellwagen wanted some of the ferries upriver destroyed, as they were being used by guerilla elements of the Nineteenth South Carolina Cavalry. The Federals found no deserters, and in fact the only trouble encountered was the shallow water farther upriver.

Within weeks, the war would be over, and the former blockaders would find themselves in the roles of peacekeepers and policemen until the army stepped in to take control. Just as they had been a controlling presence along the coast for four long years, the Federal navy would spend the final days watching and waiting, until the ships were decommissioned and the sailors sent home. During the war, however, the sparsely populated area between Georgetown and Little River had been a significant haven for blockade runners and a busy theatre for the Federal navy, as well.

THE BLOCKADERS AND BLOCKADE RUNNERS TODAY

Today, there are no obvious physical remains or reminders of the blockaders or the blockade runners, other than the boilers of the USS *Harvest Moon* (addressed in its own chapter), and whatever remains lie lost on the Atlantic floor or elsewhere. As an article in the August 28, 2008 edition of the newspaper the *Coastal Observer* noted, shipwrecks may be found in unexpected places today. In that article, Christopher Amer, an underwater archaeologist with the South Carolina Institute of Archaeology and Anthropology's maritime research division, said of one shipwreck, "If we don't find it in the water, it might be under South Island or North Island somewhere…given the level of sea shift and other factors…parts of it could be buried up to 30 feet." According to that article, there is, in fact, an 1855 shipwreck apparently on or under South Island, and this illustrates the difficulty of locating remains today.

As in the case of the *Harvest Moon*, which went down in shallow water in 1865—so shallow that most of its two upper decks were above water—time and tide have altered the site considerably; now, only a few feet of the tall boiler stack protrude above the water, and the rest of the wreck is covered by mud. As most of the beached blockade runners, such as the *Queen of the Wave*, the *Rose*, the *Golden Liner* and the *Rover*, were burned to prevent capture, only charred remains would exist under the sands. Modern sightseers will have to content themselves with a glimpse of the *Harvest Moon*'s boilers if they seek landmarks relating to the maritime adventures on the Strand during the war.

CHAPTER SIX

"WELL-CONSTRUCTED, AND VERY FORMIDABLE"

Battery White, Fort Wool and Frazier's Point

E ven before the Civil War officially began, across the South forts were constructed in anticipation of the conflict that everyone knew was sure to come. The South Carolina coast from Georgetown to Little River was no different, and on the southern end of the district, earthworks were constructed to establish a firm defensive perimeter that was designed not only to keep ships away from Georgetown but also out of Winyah Bay. By 1861, there were forts defending Georgetown at the mouths of the North and South Santee Rivers and on North, South and Cat Islands. Confederate officials believed that South Carolina would be invaded either at Hilton Head or Georgetown because the Union navy wanted a safe anchorage within striking distance of Charleston. Winyah Bay was not only large enough to harbor the entire United States Navy in 1861, but it also provided access to the Black, Pee Dee, Waccamaw and Sampit Rivers. In Georgetown, Colonel Arthur Middleton Manigault, a local man who owned a plantation on the Santee, was in charge of the area then known as the First Military District, and as such, he had nearly three thousand men at his disposal. However, after the Federals invaded and captured Hilton Head in November 1861, Manigault's force was reduced to one thousand men by December.

On March 14, 1862, Brigadier General John C. Pemberton was placed in overall command of the district, and one of his first decisions was to strip the area defenses and concentrate the majority of his available forces in Charleston. He wrote to Colonel Manigault on March 25:

Having maturely considered the subject, I have determined to withdraw the forces from Georgetown, and therefore to abandon the position…You will proceed with all the infantry force under your command to this city, Charleston, and report to Brigadier General Ripley.

Colonel Manigault was shocked. In addition to the largest regiment of infantry in the district (the Tenth South Carolina), he was to remove most of the cavalry, all of the guns and ordnance stores and, in essence, everything of military value. The man who succeeded Manigault as commander of the First District, Colonel Robert F. Graham of the Twenty-first South Carolina, was to remain in Georgetown with his troops, but by April 10, they would be transferred out as well. With the exception of the locally raised Waccamaw Light Artillery and a couple of companies of the state troops that would later become part of the Fourth and Seventh South Carolina Cavalries, the district was virtually undefended by mid-April 1862. In addition to the troop withdrawals, most of the area forts, all of which were finished or nearly finished, were abandoned and left un-garrisoned. The forts had their guns removed and replaced with painted logs, called Quaker guns, so that it at least appeared that the installations were still heavily fortified. Eventually, twenty guns from the district forts were removed and sent up the Pee Dee River to the Northeastern Railroad bridge, where they were transferred to railroad cars and shipped to Charleston.

As Colonel Manigault knew, it was a drastic decision and an impossible task for the few remaining troops. He later wrote:

So far as General Pemberton's orders applied to myself and my regiment, I did not regret the change, for we were all anxious for one…but knowing his intention as to the abandonment of this most productive grain-growing country, believing that its loss would be very seriously felt by the Confederacy in one way or another, and knowing that the destruction of the batteries and the removal of the troops would prove an invitation to the enemy too strong and too important to be resisted, the whole country lying at the mercy of a single gunboat, I took leave of my old district rather low in spirits, and with a strong presentment of coming evil.

It didn't take the Federals long to grasp the situation, and they soon took action. Colonel Manigault, who was by then far from Georgetown, later heard about conditions in Georgetown and wrote that, just as he had believed in April:

> *Whoever occupied Georgetown had control of these rivers as well as the Santee River to some degree, meaning that the possessor had a great degree of control in South Carolina. For that reason, it should have come as no surprise when the Federal Navy began to probe upriver, giving many area troops their first real taste of what was to come. My forebodings were soon verified. A few weeks after we left, two U.S. gunboats entered the bay, and proceeded to Georgetown and up the neighboring rivers, and carried off many Negroes, destroyed much property, and created great alarm. These visits were repeated several times, and on the Santees like raids were undertaken by the enemy. Those of the planters who were able to do so removed their Negroes and such property as could conveniently be transported into the interior or out of reach of the enemy, their plantations abandoned and the growing crops left to perish in the fields.*

The first of these Union forays into the area took place on May 21, 1862. On that date, the USS *Albatross*, commanded by George A. Prentiss, and the steamer USS *Norwich*, commanded by Lieutenant J.M. Duncan, entered Winyah Bay. Passing North Island, they noted that the redoubt and lighthouse were deserted, but they could see "on South Island quite an extensive fortification, with apparently several large guns mounted en barbette." Upon approaching the fort, they saw that it was deserted and that the cannons were actually Quaker guns. From South Island, they could see that the Cat Island fort had been deserted and armed with Quaker guns as well. Knowing now that the bay was undefended, on May 22, the *Albatross* and the *Norwich* steamed into Georgetown.

As the Union ships approached the wharves, their "guns within 30 yards of the houses," Confederate Major William P. Emanuel and his men set fire to the turpentine-laden brig *Joseph* and set it adrift. This attempt to drive back the Union ships failed, and the Federal ships approached the town unimpeded. Surprisingly, no exchange of gunfire took place, even with both forces in such proximity to each other, but both commanders had excellent reasons for holding their men in check. Major Emanuel knew that he was "not prepared to offer them an effectual resistance while they remain[ed] on their boats," and even though a Georgetown woman rushed to the

The USS *Norwich. U.S. Navy Historical Center illustration.*

belfry of a church and taunted the Federals by unfurling a Confederate flag, Commander Prentiss felt that "a contest in the streets would have compelled me to destroy the city, involving the ruin of the innocent with the guilty," and therefore he did not retaliate. Later that afternoon, however, the two Union ships went about ten miles up the Waccamaw River and raided a mill, carrying off eighty slaves in the process.

Soon, the Federals occupied or had destroyed the forts that the Confederates had abandoned, giving them control of and access to Winyah Bay, Georgetown and the neighboring rivers. Already, it was all too obvious that Pemberton's stripping of Confederate defenses in the area had been a grievous error. Other than Fort Randall at Little River, the area defenses consisted of a system of interior camps from which the cavalry units operated, setting out in the direction of any emergency that might arise. These, however, afforded no protection from Union ships, and instead only allowed the Confederates to react to, not prevent, Union attacks.

By August 3, Pemberton himself had visited Georgetown to select a site on which to build new forts that would defend Georgetown and block access to all of the area's rivers. Since the original forts on North, South

The Civil War from Georgetown to Little River

and Cat Islands were now in Federal possession, Pemberton selected Mayrant's Bluff and Frazier's Point for the site of the new forts. These two positions were across the bay from each other, and as such, any Federal ships attempting to enter the lower bay once the forts were completed would be caught in a murderous crossfire. Additionally, plans were made to strengthen the interior defenses along the major rivers while the large forts were being built, and this would hopefully enable the planters to reach a level of productivity unseen since the Federals began patrolling the rivers.

The area residents, especially the plantation owners, couldn't see the forts built fast enough. Even South Carolina governmental officials were clamoring for help, as the planters made up a large and influential block of wealthy voters. One move that made the local citizenry happy came when General Pemberton was promoted to lieutenant general and sent to the west to command the Department of Mississippi. In his stead, General P.G.T. Beauregard was placed in command of the Department of South Carolina, Georgia and Florida. Beauregard was well liked in South Carolina, and he certainly knew how to deal with local officials more tactfully than had the irascible Pemberton. Beauregard wrote to Governor Francis Pickens on October 8, 1862, about the state of affairs around Georgetown and assured Pickens that he had "already given orders for the construction of a battery of five or six pieces of artillery (32 pounders and rifled guns) at Mayrant's, for the defense of Winyah Bay." He noted, however, that he would only be able to garrison it with 350 men, but considering the situation in Georgetown, this would have been more than welcomed.

Assessing the situation in the Horry-Georgetown district, Beauregard decided that it was necessary to place an officer in charge who would carry enough clout to unite the many independent companies of cavalry and artillery stationed in the district and who could soothe the ruffled feathers of local planters as well. Beauregard decided to give the command of the area to a man who was not only a friend and West Point classmate of his but was also familiar with the local people and the region. The man Beauregard selected was Brigadier General James Heyward Trapier, a native of Georgetown.

General Trapier was born at Windsor Plantation on the Black River in 1815, and although he graduated from West Point third in the class of 1838 (Beauregard graduated second), he had shown little military aptitude to confirm his high standing. Early in the war, Trapier had been involved

As a Georgetown native, Confederate general James Heyward Trapier served the district capably during the years he was stationed in Georgetown. He is buried there at Prince George Church. *Civil War Photograph Collection, Library of Congress.*

in building the defenses of Charleston, and as a major of engineers, he apparently had few equals. For his work, he was praised by both Beauregard and General Roswell Ripley, and Governor Pickens said that he was "by far the most accomplished and scientific engineer we have." Had he perhaps stayed within his capacity as an engineer, history may have looked upon him more favorably, but after he was commissioned a brigadier general on October 21, 1861, his shortcomings as a leader came to light.

General Trapier's first assignment was to command the District of Eastern and Middle Florida, but he soon fell into disfavor with many of the people with whom he had to deal. While evacuating Amelia Island, he lost twenty guns to the Federal forces, an act that gave his detractors the opportunity to introduce a movement in the Florida state senate to have him removed from command. His next assignment was leading first a brigade and then, briefly, a division in the Confederate army in the west. There, he quickly fell into disfavor with his superior, General Braxton Bragg, who harshly censured him and labeled him "unsuited for…responsible positions." Citing ill health, Trapier asked to be relieved of command, although this was apparently his way of avoiding a formal dismissal. He was then ordered back to Charleston, a supernumerary whose days as an effective field officer appeared to be over.

But Beauregard felt that Trapier was well suited for the job he had in mind, and in fact, Trapier would prove to be quite capable, serving in the area for most of the remainder of the war. Upon his arrival, however, Trapier was appalled by conditions in the district. He soon found that he had fewer than six hundred men in his command, and many of these were the sick in hospitals and the walking wounded. Almost immediately, Trapier began pleading for additional troops and would continue to do so for the remainder of the war. In fact, almost every extant letter written by Trapier to his superiors is filled with pleas for more troops, artillery and supplies. He was able to get for Mayrant's Bluff a company of the Second South Carolina Artillery under the command of Captain Frederick F. Warley and a company of cavalry. These troops did most of the construction work on the fort at night on the advice of General Thomas Jordan, Confederate chief of staff, who wrote on October 19 that "sham works should be attempted at some point while in view of the [Federal] gunboats, and meanwhile the real works should be vigorously prosecuted at night."

The Federals weren't fooled, however, and on November 11, two Federal gunboats started firing on the fort. Captain Warley's men returned their fire with the nine pieces of artillery by then mounted there. After a few minutes, the Federals retired, but it was by now apparent to all that the Federals were aware of the work being done at that site. On November 21, Federal Naval Commander J.C. Beaumont of the USS *Sebago* noted that construction was under way at Mayrant's Bluff and that he had been informed that more artillery pieces were expected soon. There were two things that Trapier's new fort didn't have, however: enough men to properly man it and the large guns he felt he would need to fight off a full-scale Union attack.

General Beauregard had written to Colonel James Chestnut in Columbia on November 10 and ordered a regiment of state troops to Trapier's position to man the "batteries until other forces can be sent in that direction." Even though he was desperate for troops, Trapier was appalled at the state militia he was sent. On November 17, Trapier noted that they "arrived without arms and without ammunition. These troops

General P.G.T. Beauregard was well liked in South Carolina, and as such, he was well suited to be commander of the military district that included that state. *National Archives photograph.*

are, besides, Reserves, and in service for only ninety days. It is questionable whether they can be rendered efficient in that time, even if well armed and equipped. At present they are literally worth nothing at all." Beauregard replied to Trapier that he would send him the arms and ammunition, but those were the only troops he could spare.

Trapier also wanted big guns: Columbiads. Beauregard wrote to Trapier in December, saying that he agreed that Trapier could use the guns and that he had approved his application but no such guns were available. What Beauregard got instead was rhetoric from his superiors, to the effect that he would be better served to construct "detached batteries of two or three guns, well protected by traverses, so as to form a separate chamber for each gun, and the batteries 100 or 200 yards apart." Trapier was to be sent "two light pieces, to be put in position on Frazier's Point, opposite Mayrant's Bluff. One 12 pounder smoothbore and one rifled gun (Blakely) both on siege carriages have been ordered." In other words, Trapier wasn't going to get the Columbiads, and he would have to make do with lesser guns instead.

This page: The two ten-inch Columbiads that General Trapier worked so hard to get were never used to defend the battery, as they arrived too late in the war. Both are still there today. *Photographs courtesy of Scott Lawrence.*

Trapier ordered the Waccamaw Light Artillery posted at Frazier's Point, where it was initially planned that a sister fort to the one on Mayrant's Bluff would be built, but construction was halted at some point in order to finish the one at Mayrant's Bluff first. The Mayrant's Bluff position was more or less complete by February 1863 and was designated Battery White. On February 3, Trapier reported that Warley's fifty-three men were there manning nine guns and that the Waccamaw Light Artillery was stationed at the Frazier's Point earthworks. Consequently, by March, the total allotment of troops in the area also included four companies of the Fourth South Carolina Cavalry under Major William P. Emanuel, and Company A of the Seventh South Carolina Cavalry under the command of Captain John H. Tucker, which still only amounted to 336 cavalry and 142 artillery, a total of 478 men. Although these troops were thinly spread, it was hoped that with the addition of the armament at Battery White, the Federals would cease their forays up the area rivers, and in that case, perhaps some of the planters who had fled the area would return and once again begin producing the rice that was so vital to the undernourished Confederacy. But as General Manigault later wrote, it was too little, too late:

A certain amount of protection was thus again secured to the planters, but the mistake, excepting to a very limited extent, could not be corrected. [They]…lost much confidence in the wisdom of the military authorities, and not knowing how soon again they might have to flee…[the] system of labor which had hitherto existed in the cultivation of these valuable plantations could not be restored. They ceased to be productive, barely making a sufficiency for the labourers themselves. In this way, a very considerable portion of our labouring population, instead of producing as they might have done, a large amount of subsistence for our soldiers in the field, besides supplying themselves, had to be provided for from other portions of the state, at a time when the country could ill afford to spare anything in the way of food. This instance is only one of many where mismanagement on the part of the Government or its officials, by sacrificing their resources and multiplying their incumbrances, [sic] contributed to our final failure.

The Civil War from Georgetown to Little River

General Trapier knew that no matter how brave his men were, the vast amount of Federal manpower available would eventually overwhelm his troops unless he received some reinforcements. Despite appearances, Battery White was as yet without adequate firepower or troops to defend Georgetown. Although there were, by January, eleven pieces of artillery in the fort, none of the guns was large and all were insufficient if called upon to deal with ironclads. Furthermore, the gunboat CSS *Pee Dee* was nearing completion at the Confederate navy yard upriver at Mars Bluff, and if the Federals succeeded in capturing Battery White, they would easily be able to ascend to the navy yard and destroy the *Pee Dee* before it was completed. To emphasize the need for more troops and artillery, on January 26, Trapier wrote to his headquarters in Charleston. Trapier claimed that Battery White was insufficient to defend upper Winyah Bay, much less the nearby rivers. To add further weight to his argument, he stated:

> *The Confederate navy-yard at Mars Bluff, Peedee River is assuming daily greater and greater importance. Already has there been nearly completed there a vessel of war of some magnitude...It is contemplated, as I learn, to build others, and it seems probable that important additions to our Navy will continue to be supplied from this yard as long as the war may last...its growing importance will naturally attract the attention of the enemy. It is my duty, therefore, to invite attention to the fact that the only defense for this navy-yard consists in the battery which guards the entrance to Winyah Bay...I need not refer to the armament of Battery White; the commanding general is of course aware of its weakness...I hope I shall not be considered importunate in thus again inviting the attention of the commanding general to the subject. To me it seems of no mean importance.*

But instead of reinforcements, Trapier was to yet again lose troops. On February 1, Trapier noted the desertions of the Third and Fourth South Carolina state troops, under the command of Lieutenant Colonel R.A. Rouse and Colonel J.H. Witherspoon. These men declared that their terms of enlistment were up, and as such, they were free to go. On February 17, Trapier wrote to Beauregard, lamenting conditions in the district, noting that he now had only about three hundred men in his command, and spread out over sixty miles of coastline, they would be ineffective if needed to repel a Federal invasion. In fact, Trapier had been losing troops at an alarming rate during the previous nine months. Captain Tucker's company of independent cavalry had been made Company F of the regular Seventh South Carolina Cavalry and was sent to Virginia on March 18. In March, he also lost the two companies of the Twenty-first Georgia Cavalry that had been stationed in Murrells Inlet. Company D of the Second South Carolina Artillery had already been transferred, but at least it would be replaced by Company B of the German Artillery under the command of Captain Franz Melchers in May 1863.

But Trapier was even more concerned than usual about the diminution of troops because at the same time the Union navy was getting more and more aggressive. On January 19, three Union ships were spotted patrolling just below Battery White, and by March, they were doing more than patrolling. On March 2, the Union navy landed troops below Battery White and pushed back the Confederate pickets. It pressed the issue no further, however, and this brief reconnaissance only served to agitate Trapier more; he felt it may have been made with "a view to ulterior operations." Within days, he renewed his requests for more troops and artillery.

Trapier wanted infantry, and he wanted three ten-inch Columbiads. Columbiads were large artillery pieces used mainly in seacoast fortifications such as Battery White. They were formidable guns—ten-caliber, with a projectile weight of 128 pounds and a range of over eighteen hundred yards. Trapier believed that with the Columbiads, Battery White could withstand any assault that the Union navy might mount. On March 8, he wrote that Battery White was "well-constructed and of ample dimensions" but only "feebly armed":

> It is well situated, too, at the gorge which divides the upper from lower Winyah Bay, where the width of the channel does not exceed 1400 yards. Its site likewise is commanding, having some 20 feet elevation above the ordinary high water, but were it Gibraltar, it would be useless in a conflict with plated vessels, armed as it is at present...experience has demonstrated that against ironclads it would simply be a waste of ammunition to contend with such guns as these...we want the 10-inch Columbiad. Give us but three of these, and so far as the water approach is concerned, this section of the country will have adequate protection.

Trapier wasn't finished, however, and of course he wanted troops, too:

> *One thousand men behind the entrenchments which have been constructed*
> *would be more than a match for five times their number. Is not the saving*
> *of the district from the hands of the enemy worth three 10-inch guns and*
> *one regiment of infantry?*

Neither the guns nor the men were forthcoming, and again, on March 13, he even asked the authorities in Richmond for the guns. Again, he was denied. A report in May 1864 shows the armament at Battery White to include one thirty-two-pound smoothbore, one twelve-pound smoothbore, six twenty-four-pound smoothbores, one six-pound smoothbore, three thirty-two-pound rifles, three twelve-pound rifles, and one three-and-a-half-inch Blakely—but again, no Columbiads. The Waccamaw Light Artillery had three six-pounders and one three-and-a-half-inch Blakely in place at the unfinished earthworks and trenches on Frazier's Point.

Trapier was becoming increasingly frustrated, as he seemed to lose more and more cavalry and receive a few less-mobile artillerymen in return. This lack of troops and his rapidly shrinking forces prompted him to write to Confederate chief of staff Brigadier General Thomas Jordan on March 27:

> *Under these circumstances it is obvious that a portion of the district may*
> *of necessity be abandoned to the enemy. The question arises, which shall*
> *it be? The center of the position (Winyah Bay) must of course be held;*
> *to abandon it would of course be tantamount to the abandonment of the*
> *whole. If we withdrew from Waccamaw Neck, we would throw open*
> *wide the entire line of coast from Winyah Bay to the North Carolina*
> *line. There will not be so much as a sentinel throughout the entire*
> *extent…There is a very great danger that the navigation of the Pedee and*
> *Waccamaw Rivers will be obstructed by field batteries held in the vicinity*
> *of the latter. Again the Navy Yard at Mars Bluff would, in the event of*
> *the abandonment of Waccamaw Neck, be entirely uncovered.*

But at this point in the war, it was getting hard to hold on to the men he had, even if they weren't siphoned off to another department. On October 5, 1864, Lieutenant R.P. Swann of the USS *Potomska* reported to Rear Admiral John A. Dahlgren that he had

11 privates, Company B, German Artillery, who deserted from Battery White…the deserters report great dissatisfaction among the troops, particularly the Germans, who say they would desert without an exception were they not so strictly guarded. I find the river so strongly picketed that I can give them little assistance.

Swann went on to give exact information about the battery and guns there, noting that "at Battery White there are ten guns…in the rear of the battery there is a section of artillery consisting of two rifled 12-pounders." The mention of the two guns at the rear was the first reference to what was apparently designated Fort Wool by the Confederates, a second fortified position under construction that would have controlled the ground to the rear of Battery White. Swann's information regarding the deployment of troops was quite explicit as well, and he noted that "two companies of Cavalry, commanded by Captains M.J. Kirk and Walker, are directly in the rear of Battery White…there are…two companies of cavalry on Waccamaw Neck [and] 400 men encamped 6 miles from the town." Trapier did seem at last to have a fair-sized contingent in Georgetown, though certainly not enough to repel a major invasion.

By November, Sherman's armies were advancing at an alarming rate. The same companies of artillery and cavalry that had been in the district all summer were still on duty, but one by one they would begin to be transferred out. Trapier now had 361 men and twenty-two officers, but Kirk's Rangers were gone by the nineteenth. Gaillard's Artillery also left on the nineteenth, and in fact, by November 23, Major General Sam Jones ordered Trapier to remove himself and his remaining forces to Mount Pleasant, leaving only Captain Melchers and Company B of the German Artillery to defend the district. With Trapier ordered out, by the first of the year the highest-ranking officer in the district was Captain Melchers, but by January 31, 1865, he too would be with Trapier in Hardee's army, and Lieutenant Hermann Klatte was left with a skeleton crew of the German Artillery at Battery White and was ordered to hold out for as long as possible and then withdraw.

Although now less than one company of artillery was left to defend the entire district, those men were stationed at the most crucial point as far as access to the waterways was concerned. Battery White still presented the Federals with a formidable obstacle because, at long last, Trapier had indeed received the two much-coveted ten-inch Columbiads, the large defensive guns that would make Battery White well-nigh impregnable. But even the Columbiads came too late. After the fall of Charleston on February 17, 1865, all major Southern ports were in the hands of Federal forces. Though Georgetown was hardly on a par with Wilmington or Charleston, it was nevertheless the last large port in Confederate hands in South Carolina and, for that matter, one of very few open ports in the Confederacy. The Federals quickly moved to mount an operation to take Georgetown, and just as quickly, the Confederates chose to abandon the position.

On February 20, with Union forces closing in by land and sea, Lieutenant Klatte and what was left of the men from the German Artillery finally evacuated Battery White, and the people of Georgetown were left to their own devices. On February 22, Union Admiral John Dahlgren ordered the USS *Mingoe* into Winyah Bay to investigate rumors that Battery White was abandoned, and so on the twenty-third, Commander J. Blakely Creighton did just that. He took the *Mingoe* to within a mile and a half of Battery White and then sent out boats to check for mines before proceeding. After finding no mines, Creighton brought his ship up close to the fort and fired several rounds into the compound. Confederate deserters had told the Federals that the fort was now abandoned, so Creighton expected no response and he got none.

Creighton next sent a landing party to the fort to confirm that it was completely deserted. Executive Officer J.W. Congdon led this party, and he soon reported back to Creighton that the fort was indeed abandoned. Congdon also reported that all fifteen of the artillery pieces had been spiked and rendered unusable (in a second report he claimed that there were sixteen guns) and that there were massive quantities of shot and shell but no gunpowder. Creighton noted that the fort was "well-constructed, and very formidable" and that his men "dismantled it by dismounting the guns [and] breaking the carriages." He stationed a company of fifty marines under Lieutenant S.L. Breese in the fort and then contacted Dahlgren with his findings.

On the twenty-fifth, Georgetown surrendered, and the town was occupied by six companies of marines under Lieutenant George Stoddard. On the twenty-sixth, Dahlgren himself arrived and declared martial law. The war was over for Georgetown and Battery White.

On February 28, Dahlgren finally took the opportunity to see for himself the fort about which the Federals had been so curious, and he was impressed by what he saw. "Generally it has been much underrated," he wrote,

> *but we can now understand it was well placed, well constructed, and strongly armed, so we should have had some trouble to reduce it if well manned.*
>
> *The accounts in the reports fail to convey a correct idea of its character. The site was admirably selected, not only commanding the channel, but the various roads to the town above. The principal battery looks directly on the water, well planned and executed carefully, not only with reference to a cannonade by ships, but also to assault from the water.*

Dahlgren went on to explain that there were many "admirably contrived huts...capable of holding a considerable force," as well as "ranges of stalls for horses." Dahlgren noted also that the habitations were dry and even had brick chimneys. "The whole site would have held a couple of thousand men easily," he wrote, "and our 50 marines were hardly noticeable."

The armament in the main battery was impressive. "Three 32-pounder (6.4 inches) rifles (hooped), 2 X-inch columbiads, 4 24-pounders (smooth), 2 12-pounders rifled (hooped), 1 3¾ inch (smooth)...One 24-pounder (smooth), 1 12 pounder (smooth)," wrote Lieutenant E.O. Matthews on the twenty-fourth. This gave Battery White, counting the two guns mounted in Fort Wool, a total of sixteen guns. "The whole position was so strong that, if defended by the 500 men said to have been there," Dahlgren wrote, "we should have found it a tough business, even with the force I proposed, and it is doubtful that we could have forced the rear line."

Dahlgren also elaborated on Fort Wool to the rear of Battery White:

> *In the rear was an intrenched line, with high rampart and ditch, extending 300 yards across the only practicable ground in the rear, and completely controlling the roads to the fort from the Santee and Georgetown, and between these places a dense woods was cleaned away, so as they give no cover. A 24 pounder was mounted near each extreme of this intrenchment. This line might be a thousand yards from the water battery, and the space occupied by all might be about 100 acres.*

The Civil War from Georgetown to Little River

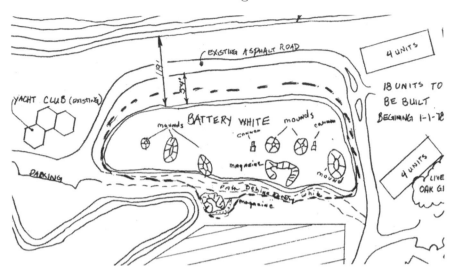

This drawing was made when Battery White was nominated for inclusion in the National Register of Historic Places in 1977. It shows that the battery remained more or less intact, but it also shows that condominiums and parking lots were encroaching on the site. The site was saved, and still looks more or less like this today. *Drawing courtesy of the South Carolina Department of Archives and History.*

In Fort Wool, there were also numerous vacant positions for guns, as it "was not entirely finished and had a 24-pounder mounted at each flank; intervening places were designed for field guns." Of the whole, Dahlgren came to the conclusion that "it is doubtful that a strong naval force could have taken it without an ironclad and a land force in reverse."

It seems that Trapier's fortification had become the near-impregnable bastion that he had envisioned, right down to the long-awaited ten-inch Columbiads. Dahlgren seemed to confirm that had Trapier been given the men he desired, it would have taken a long and bloody siege to subdue Battery White. Yet, quickly, painlessly and bloodlessly, Battery White had fallen. Perhaps it was best that this needless effusion of blood never occurred because by the time the battery was ready, the war was effectively, if not officially, over, and had been for some time. Yet Battery White stands as perhaps the one truly well-constructed fort built along what is now the Grand Strand, conceptualized, designed and built on a level with the best Confederate fortifications along the Atlantic coast.

This page and next: In addition to the two Columbiads that are still on-site at Battery White, these three guns were removed from Battery White and relocated in the Georgetown area. The gun on the concrete base is at the National Guard Armory on Highway 17, and the two on brick pedestals are in the waterfront park in Georgetown on Front Street. *Photographs by the author.*

BATTERY WHITE TODAY

Battery White is the most complete and accessible of the many Civil War landmarks that can be found along the Grand Strand today. While the earthworks and trenches that were begun on Frazier's Point are in a protected area and almost inaccessible, and the area to the rear of Battery White where Fort Wool was located was long ago bulldozed and built over, a fairly significant portion of Battery White still exists. With nearly five hundred feet of earthworks remaining, the site is maintained

The United Daughters of the Confederacy monument at Battery White. *Photograph courtesy of Scott Lawrence.*

The second of the seven nineteenth-century artillery pieces in Georgetown today that may or may not have been posted at one of the area forts during the war. This badly corroded gun sits in front of the Veterans of Foreign Wars building on Highway 17 in Georgetown, and its origins are obscure and unknown. *Photograph by the author.*

as part of a condominium complex at the location of what was originally Belle Isle Plantation. Battery White was listed in the National Register of Historic Places on November 16, 1977, so the remaining earthworks are now protected.

The earthworks are quite extensive, and one can see the remains of bombproofs, powder magazines and even a brick structure that predates the fort but was no doubt used by the Confederates as well. There is also a United Daughters of the Confederacy memorial marker at the site that was dedicated in 1929, and the coup de grace is that the two ten-inch Columbiads for which Trapier begged and pleaded are still there today. They have been mounted on concrete gun mounts and are truly impressive as they sit overlooking the bay, much as they did 150 years ago. In addition, three other cannons that were once at Battery White are still in the Georgetown area, two downtown in a waterside park on Front Street and one at the National Guard Armory at Highway 17 between Georgetown and McClellanville. Consequently, a ten- to fifteen-minute drive will allow visitors to see Battery White and five of the original sixteen guns found there in February 1865. It is a trip worth taking.

CHAPTER SEVEN

"A VESSEL OF WAR OF SOME MAGNITUDE"

The Confederate Gunboat CSS Pee Dee

Records indicate that during the Civil War, somewhere between fifty and one hundred vessels saw service along the area of the South Carolina coast from Georgetown to Little River, and that only takes into account those documented. There were blockade runners and blockaders, Federal gunboats that patrolled the district and a few Confederate warships that were occasionally stationed in the area as well. However, of all the ships that would have a bearing on wartime operations in the district, the ship that arguably had the most impact was the Confederate gunboat CSS *Pee Dee.* Even while under construction, the *Pee Dee* caused consternation among the Federals, and it was seen by the Confederates as a possible solution to breaking the blockade around Georgetown and thus as the savior of the plantations and the economy in the area. Considering the apprehension and anxiety that the ship caused the Federals, it is perhaps ironic that the ship never actually made it as far downriver as Georgetown at all. The shattered timbers of the *Pee Dee* that rested at the bottom of the river a short time after the ship was launched, and after firing but a single burst from its formidable artillery, attest to the fact that the CSS *Pee Dee* was clearly a ship of unrealized potential.

The Confederacy performed miracles when the war began, raising an army where essentially none had existed. By inducting state's troops and militia units, and training them under the many experienced Southerners who had served in the military, in many ways the Southern troops were able to stand as equals to the Union army on battlefields across the nation—as the South's early victories in the field attest. Starting a navy from scratch was

One of the propellers from the CSS *Pee Dee. Photograph courtesy of Warren Cockfield.*

another matter altogether, and though the Confederate navy would win its share of victories, it would never have enough ships or men. The seizure of ports by the Federals early in the war also made it impossible to have enough sites on the coast where it could actually build ships when needed. After the Federals recaptured the Norfolk navy yard in 1862, the Confederates were desperate for new locations to build warships. With a diminishing number of ports in Confederate hands as the war went on—and the likelihood that there would be fewer still—the Confederates turned their attention to the numerous rivers throughout the South.

Many rivers, such as those that emptied into Winyah Bay in Georgetown, provided sea access, and thus ships could be built upriver and head to sea when ready. In addition, when possible, it was helpful if the site was in proximity to a railroad in order to facilitate the transfer of materials and supplies. Stephen R. Mallory, secretary of the Confederate navy, ordered site inspections across the South to find possible locations for inland Confederate navy yards. In August 1862, one of his inspectors, Annapolis graduate Lieutenant Alphonse Barbot, recommended Mars Bluff, South Carolina, which was just up the Pee Dee River from Winyah Bay and was near a Wilmington and Manchester line railroad bridge. The river itself, with an average depth of eight feet all the way to Georgetown, would provide that much-needed ocean access once Confederate ships were completed. In addition to Mars Bluff, locations in Virginia (Richmond), Georgia (Saffold and Columbus), North Carolina (Edward's Ferry and Whitehall), Mississippi (Yazoo City), Alabama (Selma, Montgomery and Oven Bluff) and Louisiana (Shreveport) were chosen as well.

Of course, if the river provided ocean access to the Confederates once they completed ships at Mars Bluff, then that also meant that any Federal ships would have access to the navy yard if they chose to foray upriver from Winyah Bay. At Mars Bluff, that was a viable threat. Already in 1862, Federal gunboats had discovered that the forts below Georgetown, the largest of which was at Cat Island, had been stripped of artillery. As soon as the discovery was made, as expected, the Federal gunboats began probing upriver when possible. However, in the case of the Pee Dee River and the navy yard at Mars Bluff, the Confederates had provided for its defense. The Confederates had blocked the river with rafts, and the site for the yard and its defense were well chosen. General W.W. Harllee reported to General John Pemberton that there the bluff was

> *40 feet high, almost perpendicular, and the river not 100 yards wide. On the eastern bank for miles the swamp is low, marshy, and impenetrable…it would be impossible to harm the men on the bluffs by shells from the boats or even to land with any sort of resistance…there are two cannons (18 and 12 pounders), planted securely in batteries dug down, and leaving the solid earth 50 feet in front…to attempt* [to attack] *the site will expose the men there to certain destruction from our large guns and small arms.*

With the site chosen and preparations made for its defense, there was a sense of urgency in the Confederate communications that indicated that they wanted the ship underway as soon as possible. On December 16, 1862, Secretary Mallory wrote to Lieutenant William G. Dozier, who was in charge of operations at the site, and notified him that "the department relies on you to complete [the construction of the gunboat] in the shortest possible time…push the work on night and day." On December 24, Mallory wrote to Dozier once again, taking the opportunity to tell him that "a paymaster and constructor are on the way to Mars Bluff to report to you." He added, "Go ahead with all dispatch." A large detail of men, including Acting Naval Constructor John L. Porter, CSN, shipwrights and the support staff the navy yard would need, was soon on site, and the work began. The work would progress steadily, first directed by Lieutenant Dozier, who was succeeded in March 1863 by Lieutenant Van Renssalaer Morgan, who himself was succeeded as commander of the yard in August 1864 by Lieutenant Edward J. Means.

Perhaps some of the urgency that the Confederates felt had to do with the increased presence of the Union navy around Georgetown. While there were a few Confederate ships in the Georgetown area—the *Nina*, an armed steamer, and the *Treaty*, an old tug used to ferry troops—these ships would be no match for the Federal ships if they were inclined and able to enter the rivers in search of Confederate vessels. In May 1862, General Harllee reported that most Federal ships were "too large to navigate the Pee Dee" but that they did have two smaller light draft ships—the USS *Planter* and the USS *Darlington*—"both of which have run the river often." At some point, the enterprising Union navy would probably assemble enough ships capable of going upriver (and they in fact eventually did), so of course the first ship built at the navy yard needed to be one that could counter this threat.

Confederate General James Heyward Trapier, who was in command of the Georgetown military district for most of the war, wanted the first ship built at Mars Bluff to be an ironclad. In fact, by late 1862, the Confederate navy's policy was to build very few wooden gunboats at the inland navy yards in favor of the much-needed ironclads, but in this case, the first ship to be built at Mars Bluff was to be a wooden gunboat, the second a side-wheel steamer and the third a torpedo boat. The first built was to take the name of its river and would be christened the CSS *Pee Dee*. And while there are many aspects of the *Pee Dee*'s history that are muddled and inconclusive—even its name is called into question, as it is at times referred to as the *Pedee* and the *PeeDee*—nevertheless, its story is an interesting one.

The *Pee Dee* would be an impressive Macon-class gunboat, though there are many conflicting details about its size, equipment and armament. The official Confederate records say that it was a single-engine, double-propeller, wooden screw-sloop gunboat, 170 feet long and 26 feet wide, with a draft of 10 feet and capable of reaching a speed of nine knots. One eyewitness account from a Union spy claimed that the ship was but 150 feet in length, while newspaper articles written during the twentieth century differ even more. A *Florence Morning News* article from 1950 claims

This Confederate torpedo boat (possibly the CSS *David*) was photographed in Charleston in 1865. A November 1864 report on the Mars Bluff navy yard noted that "there is also being built at this yard a torpedo boat," but despite the fact that the boat was in progress, it was never completed. *National Archives photograph.*

that the ship was 110 feet long and 40 feet wide, while a *Columbia Record* article from 1954 claimed that the *Pee Dee* was 170 feet long with a beam of 28 feet. The official records compiled after the war say that the ship's machinery was brought from England, although a report on November 1, 1864, says that "her engines were built at Richmond, and are not of sufficient power for greater speed [than nine knots], having been provided for a smaller vessel at first, which circumstances prevented the building of." Whatever the case, the machinery was enormous and heavy, with the double propellers weighing approximately fifteen hundred pounds and the boiler weighing about forty-five tons.

Even more controversial is the disinformation concerning its armament. The final Confederate records compiled after the war claimed that its battery consisted of "four 32 pounders and two pivots," but clearly this was never the case, though perhaps it was intended at one time. A Confederate report dated November 30, 1863, claimed that it had five guns; a report of April 30, 1864, records it as having three guns; and yet another report of November 1, 1864, claimed that "she mounts a battery of five guns. Three of which are mounted on pivots." It may be possible that at different times before it was launched the *Pee Dee* was intended to mount different numbers of guns and that these numbers changed as the guns intended for the ship were sent to other places—a problem faced by the Confederacy more and more frequently as the war went on. Yet Federal reports listed it as having even more guns. On October 29, 1864, Admiral John Dahlgren wrote to Commander N.B. Harrison on the USS *Canandaigua*, "I have been informed that the Rebels have built a Gunboat on the 'Peedee,' which may be expected to come down as soon as the river is high enough. She is said to be of light draft, and to carry eight guns, of which two are ten inch. The account may be exaggerated but it is well to be prepared."

Contrary to the Federals' information, when launched, its armament consisted of one 6.4-inch Brooke rifle and one 7.0-inch thirty-two-pound Brooke rifle, one on a pivot at the bow and the other at the stern. The other artillery piece was a pivoted 9-inch Dahlgren gun mounted amidships. Considering that the 6.4-inch Brooke rifle was roughly twelve feet long and weighed ninety-one-hundred pounds, the 7.0-inch Brooke rifle was more than twelve feet long and weighed fifteen thousand pounds and the 9.0-inch Dahlgren gun was about eleven feet long and weighed ten thousand pounds, even with only three guns the *Pee Dee* mounted an impressive array of artillery.

This photo shows Union seamen manning a Dahlgren gun, the type that was found on the *Pee Dee*. This gun was ironically named for the Union admiral who was bent on destroying the Confederate ship. *National Archives photograph.*

The Civil War from Georgetown to Little River

From the time the navy yard was constructed, there were periodic reports on the ship's progress. On November 30, 1863, the ship was reported as "advancing to completion" and its "machinery [was] ready." On January 26, 1864, General Trapier reported that in his estimation the ship would be ready in two months. Trapier's guess was extremely optimistic, but this was perhaps due to his use of the Mars Bluff navy yard and the construction of the *Pee Dee* as an inducement to try and wrest more troops and artillery from the Confederate government for the defense of the area—a tactic that he would use often. On February 17, 1864, Trapier said that unless he was given more troops to defend the forts on Winyah Bay,

> *the navy yard at Mars Bluff would be exposed to almost certain destruction. For even supposing* [Union] *boats should not be able to navigate the river so high up, a few hundred cavalry, landed on its banks 20 or 30 miles below, could by a sudden dash complete the work of destruction in a very few hours.*

Again, on March 13, he used this approach, writing to General P.G.T. Beauregard and General Samuel Cooper, adjutant and inspector general:

> *Incidentally, it may not be amiss for me to mention that upon our defenses* [in Georgetown and Winyah Bay] *rests the safety of the Confederate navy yard at Mars Bluff. Should the enemy break over our line of defense, 100 cavalry landed on the banks of the Pedee would in a few hours reach the navy-yard, complete the work of destruction there, and return without encountering any serious obstacle, because there would not be time to throw one in their way, if they moved promptly.*

This land-based attack never came, but clearly the *Pee Dee* was in fact nearing a point of completion. On April 30, 1864, it was listed as having a commander in place, Confederate naval Lieutenant Oscar Johnson, a graduate of the United States Naval Academy and previously an instructor at the Confederate Naval Academy onboard the school ship *Patrick Henry*. Johnson had been sent to Mars Bluff with a contingent of ninety men and officers to assume command of the warship when it was ready to be launched. It was also planned that a company of Confederate marines be assigned to the ship, and Marine Second Lieutenant Ruffin Thomson of Mississippi wrote to his parents, telling them that he expected to be assigned to the *Pee Dee*. While there is no evidence to suggest that the marines were duly assigned, with a crew of more than one hundred and the ship's impressive firepower, the *Pee Dee* would be a formidable foe indeed for the Federal ships around Georgetown.

By November 1864, the *Pee Dee* seemed about ready to run out, as a report on November 1 noted that the *Pee Dee* "has just been completed." In addition, underway and already "on the stocks" was "a small side-wheel steamer intended for transport on the Pedee River, for grain and other provisions for the government and any other necessary purposes." Work had progressed far enough along that "the machinery of this vessel has been provided for." Finally, the report noted that "there is also being built at this yard a torpedo boat," and so it looked as if the *Pee Dee*, when launched, would soon have some company.

The Federals were certainly worried. On October 29, Admiral Dahlgren had written to Commander N.B. Harrison on the *Canandaigua*, ordering him to report to Winyah Bay and relieve Commander George Balch and the USS *Pawnee*. At that time, he was to give Balch the order to "take position in the channel and prevent [the *Pee Dee*] from getting out to sea." Dahlgren had certainly chosen the right ship to fight the *Pee Dee* if that became necessary. The *Pawnee* was 221 feet long and 47 feet wide, with a 10-foot draft and capable of reaching a maximum speed of ten knots. The crew of 181 manned an impressive array of firepower—two twelve-pounders, eight nine-inch smoothbores, one one-hundred-pound Parrot rifle, four nine-inch Dahlgren smoothbores and two other smaller guns—giving the ship by far the most firepower of any Federal ship in the district.

When the CSS *Pee Dee* was launched early in 1865, hundreds of people attended the ceremony as it slid into the waters of the Pee Dee River. Among those in attendance were Southerners who were Union sympathizers spying for the Federals, and on January 31, Commander J. Blakely Creighton of the USS *Mingoe*, stationed off of Georgetown, received two Georgetown men under a flag of truce. These men told Creighton that they had come to give him information about the "vessel of war at the river," meaning, of course, the *Pee Dee*. They stated that one of the two men had actually been onboard the ship and that the ship was

> *a wooden vessel one hundred and fifty feet in length with a crew of one hundred men, that she is in commission and ready to come down but has*

not done so yet, is waiting for orders. She has an armament of three guns-pivot, all rifles-two Brook[e]s 32 pr, and one Whitworth. The caliber he did not know. The water is still high enough in the river for her to come down, and he thinks will be so for several days.

The construction of the *Pee Dee* had taken so long from conception to completion that now that it was actually available for duty, the Confederacy's days were numbered. The Federals had assembled a large fleet in Georgetown, and other ships were on the way. General Trapier feared the worst, and on January 26, wrote to Brigadier General Thomas Jordan that even with fifteen artillery pieces, Battery White, which had been built in 1863 and was now the primary fortification guarding the mouth of the Pee Dee River and protecting Georgetown, was insufficient to defend upper Winyah Bay and the nearby rivers. To add further weight to his argument, he stated:

The Confederate navy-yard at Mars Bluff, Peedee River is assuming daily greater and greater importance. Already has there been nearly completed there a vessel of war of some magnitude...It is contemplated, as I learn, to build others, and it seems probable that important additions to our Navy will continue to be supplied from this yard as long as the war may last...its growing importance will naturally attract the attention of the enemy. It is my duty, therefore, to invite attention to the fact that the only defense for this navy-yard consists in the battery which guards the entrance to Winyah Bay.

Even on the day the letter was written, it was already too late. On January 24, Lieutenant Commander Barnes of the USS *Bat* noted that the USS *Mingoe* was now inside Winyah Bay and Georgetown was "effectively closed." By February 24, the Federals would learn from Confederate deserters that Battery White had been abandoned without a fight. The Federals therefore had Winyah Bay blockaded, held Battery White and Georgetown (which surrendered on the twenty-fifth) and, in addition, General Sherman's invading troops were reported to be just twelve miles away from Georgetown. The *Pee Dee* was trapped upriver with no way to get out.

On February 26, the CSS *Pee Dee* completed its one and only mission successfully by covering the retreat of General Hardee's troops as they crossed the Pee Dee River at Cheraw. These were, in fact, some of the last Confederate troops in the state, and among them were General Trapier and the last fourteen officers and 170 men he had remaining from the nearly 3,000 men who had originally been detailed to defend the Georgetown to Little River area of South Carolina in 1861. Even as the *Pee Dee* covered the retreat, Sherman's troops were on the outskirts of Cheraw.

In addition, although the Confederate prison camp in nearby Florence had been abandoned in February and those still living of its twelve thousand Federal prisoners had been transferred to Greensboro, North Carolina, many of Sherman's troops advancing up from Georgia were not aware of the transfer. Nearby Florence was a constant target of Federal raids. In late February, Union troops of the Fifteenth Illinois Cavalry headed for Florence to free the prisoners and were turned back by the Fifth South Carolina Cavalry, but another attempt was soon forthcoming. In early March, another force of Federals attempted to enter Florence. Men of the Seventh and Ninth Illinois, the Twenty-ninth Missouri Mounted Infantry and the Fifteenth Army Corps foragers under the command of Colonel Ruben Williams got to within two miles of Florence before Confederate cavalry, under General Joe Wheeler and Colonel John Colcock, turned them back. Colonel Williams's men, while unable to take the town, were able to destroy a great deal of supplies that the Confederates needed quite badly. Soon, these Confederate troops would also leave the area.

As a result, with its lone mission successfully completed, and as the last of the Confederate authorities left the region and contact was broken with Richmond, the *Pee Dee* was more or less trapped on a tiny stretch of river in an area completely surrounded by hostile forces. By early March, the ship's officers had three choices: try to fight their way out at Georgetown, surrender to the Union authorities or destroy the ship. It probably wasn't a hard decision to make. The Pee Dee River was too low to provide the ship with an ocean access, so essentially trying to take the vessel to Georgetown and fight through the blockade was out of the question. The thought of surrendering such a proud and unscarred ship intact was unthinkable, so the most logical thing to do was prevent the ship from falling into Federal hands by destroying it. As with many other elements surrounding the ship, even its date of destruction is uncertain, listed variously as March 4, 15, 16 or 18. In the *Official Records*, correspondence from March 4 shows that General Sherman wrote to General H.W. Slocum from Cheraw that "there was a gunboat here…but it was blown up today about six miles down the river." Despite Sherman's claim, March 15 is generally accepted as the date of the ship's destruction.

Lieutenant Johnson and his men burned the ship. After all usable supplies and ammunition had been unloaded, a party of seven men loaded the cargo on wagons and shipped it to Cheraw; from there, the supplies were sent on to Charlotte. Before burning the ship, Lieutenant Johnson had the crew fire a single defiant shot into the woods—the only time the *Pee Dee*'s guns were ever fired in anger. After the demolition of the ship—the explosion was reportedly heard as far as thirty miles away—Lieutenant Johnson and his men decided to head inland and join up with other Confederate units, including General Joseph Johnston's army in North Carolina. Clearly, they knew that they would not be returning to Mars Bluff, as in addition to destroying the *Pee Dee*, the navy yard was burned, and Midshipman William F. Clayton later recalled that a "river steamer built [t]here and a steam launch were sunk and the command moved on to join the army." A letter from Flag Officer William Hunter dated March 25, 1865, noted that Second Lieutenant J.R. Price and Midshipman Clayton reported to Hunter on orders of Lieutenant Johnson, "late in command of *C.S.S. Peedee*, which vessel I learn had been destroyed." Lieutenant Price was reassigned to the CSS *Sampson* and Clayton to the CSS *Macon*, but by this point even the most optimistic of Confederates must have realized that the end was very near.

Indeed, just a few weeks later it was all over. For all the concern on the part of the Federals and hope on the part of the Confederates, the *Pee Dee* had never become a factor in the war in the district. The charred timbers of the ship sank to the bottom of the river, where they would remain unseen for another fifty-five years, at which time the ship would become the focus of interest, pride and controversy all over again.

The CSS *Pee Dee* Today

The *Pee Dee*'s history since the Civil War has been perhaps more eventful than its actions during the war. In September 1925, a drought led to the burned hulk of the ship being exposed for the first time since the war. According to the *Florence Morning News* of September 15, 1925, hundreds of people traveled through the swamp to see the ship. Its "propellers and

SOUTH CAROLINA

CONFEDERATE NAVY YARD

The Confederacy established a
navy yard ¼ mile NW about 1863
on the banks of the
Great Pee Dee River.
Here, under the command of
Lt. Van Renssalaer Morgan,
a wooden gunboat,
the C.S.S. Pee Dee, was built.
Launched by November 1864, it was
burned to prevent its capture by
Federal forces in March 1865.

A historical marker noting the site of the Confederate navy yard at Mars Bluff. *Photograph by the author.*

boiler are plainly visible as is a large portion of the deck. The propellers are of iron or steel. The old boiler is a tremendous affair…both the boiler and propellers are in a good state of preservation," the paper reported. Local chapters of the United Daughters of the Confederacy sent a telegram to the governor, claiming that the wreck was being "mutilated by souvenir hunters" and asking for permission to take custody of the wreck. Permission was granted, and eventually the propellers were removed and mounted at the Florence Library and then, later, at the Florence Museum, where they sit today on concrete pedestals. There is also a granite marker there with a bas-relief of the ship that provides details relating to the ship and its destruction.

In 1954, low water again exposed the remains of the ship, and a portion of the wreck was salvaged and put on display on the west bank of the river on Highway 301 as a tourist attraction, though commercially the venture was a failure. In 1958, U.S. Navy divers attempted to locate the ship's cannons but were unsuccessful. In 1961, some of the wreck, including a section of the stern and the boiler, was removed to launch a tourist attraction called "Confederateland" in Dillon County, and apparently that venture also failed. Ultimately, the remains of the *Pee Dee* raised in 1954 fell victim to their inability to attract tourism dollars, and according to Ted Gragg, leader of the team that worked under the supervision of the South Carolina Institute of Technology and Archaeology, the wooden remains were used as landfill for the gully that Highway 95 bridged in front of South of the Border near Dillon, and the boiler "remained in

The Civil War from Georgetown to Little River

This page: These two pictures, taken in the 1950s, show the boiler and a shattered section of the timbers from the CSS *Pee Dee* after they had been pulled from the Pee Dee River and placed in a field near Highway 301. Both were later transported to Dillon and then eventually discarded as waste. *Photographs courtesy of Tom Kirkland©.*

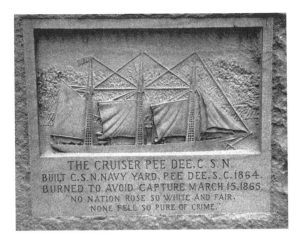

This page: At the Florence Museum, a bas-relief marker and the *Pee Dee*'s mounted propellers commemorate the ship. Several of the dates on the pedestals and marker are incorrect. *Photographs courtesy of Warren Cockfield.*

a Latta junkyard until 1989 or so when the yard's contents were sold for scrap." Interestingly, the cannonball that the *Pee Dee* defiantly fired before the ship was destroyed was recovered by the Marion chapter of the United Daughters of the Confederacy.

According to the University of South Carolina's Maritime Research Division, in 1996, a team received permission to dive on and survey the site of the navy yard at Mars Bluff. The group mapped and recovered a number of artifacts from the bottom, including "artillery shells, shot, and canister, medicinal bottles, carpenter tools, and other objects." As this book went to press in July 2009, a joint project between archaeologists from the University of South Carolina and East Carolina University was in the process of locating and raising the ship's three guns and mapping out and excavating the navy yard's fourteen buildings. Clearly, there is more to come involving the CSS *Pee Dee*.

CHAPTER EIGHT

THE EVENTFUL FINAL DAYS OF THE USS *HARVEST MOON*

Two ships figure prominently—perhaps one should say eventfully—in the annals of the Civil War along the Grand Strand. Neither of these ships were blockade runners that completed a number of successful runs into or out of the ports at Georgetown, Murrells Inlet or Little River, and neither of them were the Federal blockaders who destroyed significant amounts of Confederate goods and ships along the Strand. Instead, while the names of the more than fifty ships that actively fought the coastal war from Georgetown to Little River are now all but forgotten, the two most famous ships connected with the area had almost no wartime activity in the region. Perhaps what makes these two ships so famous is that the wrecks of both still rest there in the water, one in Winyah Bay and the other in the Pee Dee River. What further links these ships is that both had very unlucky, almost tragic endings, and they sank within days of one another in March 1865. One of those ships, the Confederate gunboat CSS *Pee Dee*, had its story told in the previous chapter. This is the story of the *Pee Dee*'s partner in misfortune, the Union warship USS *Harvest Moon*.

Like many ships that would take part in the American Civil War, the *Harvest Moon* did not begin its existence as a warship. However, unlike many other ships pressed into service, it was a newer ship and was actually launched by shipbuilder Joseph Dyer in Portland, Maine, on November 22, 1862. First owned by Spear, Lang and Delano of Boston, Massachusetts, the *Harvest Moon* was a ship of 546 tons; it was 193 feet long with a beam of 29 feet and an 8-foot draft. Its engines gave it a maximum speed of fifteen knots and an average speed of nine knots, and as a side-wheel steamer, it

This picture appears in the *Official Records* as depicting the USS *Harvest Moon*, though there is some question as to its validity because the ship in the drawing has two masts, whereas the *Harvest Moon* was only known to have had one. *U.S. Navy Historical Center illustration.*

had a vertical beam engine to power the wheel. Interestingly enough, the engine was actually salvaged from a steamer lost in the sea off of China and then recovered and sent to Halifax. Perhaps superstitious individuals (as sailors are often wont to be) would have seen this as a bad omen; as fate would have it, perhaps it was a bad omen indeed.

After a year in private service running passengers and freight between Bangor and Portland, the ship was purchased in Boston by Commodore J.B. Montgomery and was fitted out as a ship of war. When commissioned on February 12, 1864, its armament consisted of a twenty-pound Parrott rifle, four twenty-four-pound howitzers and one twelve-pound rifle. It was a rather graceful ship, and as such, it was less suited for a gunboat because it had been built for service of another kind. While in Union service, the *Harvest Moon* was to be an admiral's flagship, the admiral in this case being Rear Admiral John A. Dahlgren.

Dahlgren was a career navy man and may be best known today for his fame as a naval ordnance innovator. Dahlgren invented a number of naval artillery pieces, and for his many innovations, he has often been referred to as the "father of American naval ordnance." Dahlgren was given command

Admiral John Dahlgren onboard the USS *Pawnee*, one of the ships on station in Georgetown along with the *Harvest Moon*. Behind him is one of his famed Dahlgren guns. *U.S. Navy Historical Center photograph.*

of the South Atlantic Blockading Squadron in July 1863, and in this capacity, his job was to reduce the major Southern ports such as Charleston. As a result, his dominion extended to Georgetown and its environs as well. Of his service as commander of the South Atlantic Blockading Squadron, the Naval Historical Center's biographies section notes that though Dahlgren was a brave and capable officer, his shortcoming was that "he never figured out how to counter the enemy's underwater defenses." This would be unfortunate for Dahlgren and the crew of the *Harvest Moon*.

Once commissioned and in the area encompassing Dahlgren's command, the *Harvest Moon* was to take station around Charleston. But between the time that the *Harvest Moon* was commissioned in February 1864 and the time it would take position around Georgetown in February 1865, if its records are any indication, two things would seem to be true: it was not a happy ship, and it was not a lucky ship. In terms of the former, the captain's log noted a wide variety of disciplinary infractions over the course of the first eight weeks of the ship's commission:

> *March 4: James Mc Cue returned intoxicated and commenced breaking in 5 panels around the boiler. Confined in double irons.*
> *March 20: John Doyle (bargeman) was down in the main hold and took a hammock lashing without orders and when being spoken to by the Capt. was surly and was ordered confined in double irons.*
> *March 26: Thomas Tealy, carpenters mate confined for smuggling liquor thru the gate.*
> *April 25: Mustered all hands on quarter deck. Commenced searching baggage for $60 stolen from John B. Stanton, Marine. Found it concealed in clothing of William H. Morris (OS), confined in double irons.*
> *April 26: Confined Henry Quick dbl. irons. Presented forged pass at gate. 6 men AWOL.*

For such a new ship with a veteran crew—and an admiral's flagship at that—there seemed to be a high rate of infractions of a rather serious nature, from insubordination to theft and being absent without leave.

As for it being an unlucky ship, throughout what would be its brief career as a warship, the *Harvest Moon* seemed to have the tendency to run into and over things. The first incident of note in the captain's log for March 2, 1864, notes that it "struck ground several times" and "the ship [ran] on a mudbank." On March 16, the captain noted:

> *At 4:15am saw a schooner…struck her on the starboard quarter. Captain & Exec. officer called immediately also all hands…the ship's bow was stove in making much water…6am 2 inches of water above keelson…All pumps going constantly to keep ship free. Passed Fort Washington and at 10:45 anchored. Stopped engine and ran donkey pump.*

For the next several days, the ship was pumped constantly in order to keep it afloat, and Admiral Dahlgren had to move his pennant to the USS *Baltimore* on March 19 until he deemed the *Harvest Moon* seaworthy on March 24.

Even more problematic was its grounding a few months later on December 22, 1864, when it was stationed off of Savannah. Its passenger that night was none other than General William T. Sherman, who was onboard the *Harvest Moon* to conduct a council of war with Dahlgren. With his troops poised to take Savannah, Sherman had ordered his officers to make no moves while he was away. This was probably in order to keep overzealous officers from unadvisedly starting a major offensive because certainly he could not have foreseen his delay in returning to his command.

That night, when Sherman's conference with Dahlgren was over, the *Harvest Moon* became grounded in the mud once again and was unable to be moved until the following day. In the meantime, General William Hardee's Confederates were able to evacuate Savannah that same night, unwittingly aided by the fact that although the Federals were to some degree aware of the evacuation, they were powerless to pursue without explicit orders from Sherman. The next day, Hardee's men were gone; the grounding of the *Harvest Moon* had allowed thousands of Confederates to escape Savannah, free to fight another day. In a letter on January 1, 1865, to Chief of Staff General Henry Halleck, Sherman lamented the fact that the escape of Hardee's army, which he had hoped to trap and defeat, left him "very much disappointed." Once again, the unlucky *Harvest Moon*'s propensity to run onto things had led to disastrous results.

If a superstitious person needed anything else to make a case that the ship was unlucky, perhaps he might have pointed to the fact that its captain, John K. Crosby, had already had a date with infamy. Crosby had replaced the *Harvest Moon*'s first captain, Joshua Warren, and Crosby himself would probably be little more than a footnote in history were it not for his command before coming to the *Harvest Moon*. Crosby had been the master of the USS *Housatonic*, the Federal ship sunk by the Confederate submarine CSS *Hunley*. On the night of February 17, 1864, while anchored off of the Charleston Bar, a lookout on the *Housatonic* spotted the *Hunley*. Crosby, who was on deck at the time, tried to get his ship underway but wasn't able to do so. In one of the most notable two-ship maritime encounters of the war—perhaps second only to the battle between the *Monitor* and the *Merrimac*—the *Hunley* rammed the *Housatonic* using a torpedo attached to a spar, and the *Housatonic* went down in minutes. The *Housatonic* became the first warship ever sunk by a submarine, and so Crosby was party to one of the most infamous firsts in Union naval history. Unfortunately for Crosby, it would not be the last time he would be commander of a ship that fell victim to a first of a rather dubious distinction.

By February 1865, however, the *Harvest Moon* seemed to have been riding a streak of good luck—albeit one of just a little more than a month's duration. The Confederacy was in shambles, and as the coastal ports and fortifications were being systematically gobbled up by the Union navy, the Federals' attention turned to one of the few remaining Confederate harbors on the coast: Winyah Bay and the port of Georgetown. Because Charleston had been their main target on the South Carolina coast, it was only after it was secured that they were able to reassign the ships needed not just to blockade but to actually subdue Georgetown if needed. As far as the Federals were concerned, they probably felt that they would have to take the port by force, due to the presence of the largest military installation ever built on what is today known as the Grand Strand: Battery White.

Battery White warrants its own chapter in this book as it was indeed a formidable defensive position. Situated on Mayrant's Bluff in Winyah Bay, by February 1865 its armament was extensive, and in Dahlgren's own words, it was

> *a very formidable work, consisting of several detached batteries. In the rear was an intrenched line, with high rampart and ditch, extending 300 yards across the only practicable ground in the rear, and completely controlling the roads to the fort from the Santee and Georgetown...A 24 pounder was mounted near each extreme of this intrenchment the space occupied by all might be about 100 acres.*

The artillery at Battery White, though regarded by the Confederates as insufficient to defend Winyah Bay, was deemed impressive by the Federals. The Federals saw that taking the position by force might be difficult, as the main battery consisted of, among other guns, three 6.4-inch thirty-two-pounders, two 10-inch Columbiads, one eighteen-pound long-siege gun, one twelve-pounder siege gun and other artillery. This gave Battery White, counting the two guns mounted to the rear, a total of sixteen guns. As Dahlgren noted, "The whole position was so strong that…we should have found it a tough business" to take the fort, "and it is doubtful that we could have forced the rear line."

But Admiral Dahlgren and his men were in fact prepared to assault the fort if need be, and certainly, as they steamed into Georgetown on February 26, 1865, they must have expected to do so. But by the time they arrived that evening, Battery White had already fallen. It had been abandoned by the fleeing Confederates as the remainder of the troops in Georgetown had been ordered to link up with General Joseph Johnston's army in North Carolina. By the time Dahlgren arrived, the fort was occupied by a company of Federal marines. That same day, the town itself was garrisoned by six companies of Federal marines, and as he arrived, Admiral Dahlgren proclaimed martial law in Georgetown—to which the officials of the town agreed when they surrendered the town. With the guns of the USS *Mingoe* trained on the town and the marines in place, for the first time in four years Georgetown was under the flag of the United States of America.

With the town under Federal control, the Union navy participated in a simple mop-up operation while trying to establish contact with Sherman's troops, which were closing in from the south. Admiral Dahlgren had amassed a considerable naval force in Winyah Bay, and during the last two weeks of February and up until the first of March, in addition to the *Harvest Moon* and the *Mingoe*, the USS *Catalpa*, the USS *Chenango*, the USS *Clover*, the USS *Flambeau*, the USS *Geranium*, the USS *Mcdonough*, the USS *Nipsic*, the USS *Pawnee*, the USS *Sonoma* and the USS *Sweetbriar* were all stationed in and around Georgetown. Some of these ships explored the area's rivers, some stayed outside of the bar and some just waited so that they would be on hand if any Confederate retaliation occurred. It was an impressive flotilla, and probably as a result, few incidents of note occurred since the *Harvest Moon* had been in port. Other than seeing lights on the shore, hearing an occasional rifle shot and having to open fire on a mysterious boat that may have been a drifting derelict, it was an uneventful time for the most part. Perhaps the only ill omen had been that on the twenty-seventh, the *Harvest Moon* had run "onto a wreck off the city." Even when things were going the Union navy's way, the *Harvest Moon* had a tendency to hit things.

Early on the morning of March 1, Dahlgren ordered Crosby to get the ship underway and to head back to Charleston, as his work was seemingly done in Georgetown. At about 7:45 a.m., as Dahlgren was having breakfast in his cabin, "a loud noise occurred and the bulkhead separating the cabin from the wardroom was shattered and driven in toward me…water was coming in through a great gap in the bottom. The main deck had also been blown through." Crosby claimed that he saw "a large hole, 10 feet by 12 feet square, stove through to the main deck fifteen to twenty feet aft of the shaft on the starboard side."

At the time, no one was sure what had caused the explosion. Ensign W.H. Bullis noted that he "felt a shock," and "seeing her smokestack shake I supposed her boiler had exploded." Engineer James A. Miller noted, "I experienced a shock and saw a column of water and smoke passing up through the deck some 14 feet from where I stood. My first impression was that a shell had exploded and I thought so until I reached the deck." Patrick McGrath, who was aft washing down the deck when he "was suddenly thrown overboard" by the explosion, claimed, "I thought a gun in the gangway had burst." Even Admiral Dahlgren was confused. "My first notion was that the boilers had burst," he said, "then the smell of burnt gunpowder suggested that the magazine had exploded." None of these assessments were correct, however. This time, the *Harvest Moon* had struck not a wreck or a sandbar but a "torpedo," or what would later come to be known as a floating mine.

When the war began, in many ways it had still been a "gentleman's war," but as the conflict wore on, many of the more horrific tools of warfare that we know today were introduced, especially as the South struggled to overcome its obvious deficiency in numbers and armament. One man vilified for his innovation in mines was Brigadier General Gabriel Rains, the head of the Confederate Torpedo Bureau, and he was as famous for his development of antipersonnel mines as Dahlgren was for his innovation in naval ordnance. Rains glowingly reported to Confederate secretary of war John C. Breckinridge on March 31, 1865, "the destruction of Dahlgren's flagship the *Harvest Moon* by a torpedo near Georgetown, S.C." and indeed, it had been a "torpedo" and not a burst boiler or an overheated gun that blew a hole in the *Harvest Moon*.

The mine was not one that had been paddled up against the ship in the night; rather, it was a submerged mine that had been laid prior to the ship's arrival. The previous fall, with the Federal push coming closer and closer to Georgetown, it was obvious that it was just a matter of time until the

The Civil War from Georgetown to Little River

Brigadier General Gabriel
Rains, the head of the
Confederate Torpedo Bureau.
*Civil War Photograph Collection,
Library of Congress.*

Union navy made an assault on Battery White and the surrounding area. There were no longer any blockade runners using Winyah Bay, so as a last line of defense, the decision was made to mine the bay. This responsibility fell to Captain Thomas West Daggett of the First South Carolina Infantry, a Georgetown man who was by specialty an ordnance officer. Daggett was well acquainted with the apparatus of building mines, and after deciding to mine Winyah Bay, he chose Stephen A. Rouquie to assist him. Rouquie had formerly been a lieutenant in the Tenth Regiment Infantry but had resigned due to sickness in 1862. He recovered and reenlisted with the German Artillery, which was then stationed at Battery White.

By September, Daggett and Rouquie had constructed mines on the second floor of a store owned by the Rouquies on Front Street in Georgetown, and after the mines were built, Daggett reportedly had eighteen of them laid at strategic intervals in Winyah Bay, ready to detonate if struck by an invading Federal warship. Their work was not in vain, for the hole in the *Harvest Moon* was due to one of the water mines that Daggett and Rouquie had laid before the *Harvest Moon* arrived. Union sympathizers among the residents of Georgetown had informed the Federals about the mines at least as early as January, but as Dahlgren noted, "So much has been said in ridicule of torpedoes that very little precautions are deemed necessary, and if resorted to are probably taken with less care than if due weight was attached to the existence of these mischievous things." Consequently, though there were later claims that the bay had recently been dragged for torpedoes by the *Mingoe*, somehow this one had been missed, even though it may have been in the bay for months. Rains, in fact, claimed that it "was left there before our troops evacuated." No matter how old the mine was, it did its job well, and the *Harvest Moon* went down in less than five minutes; by most accounts, it sank in less than two and a half minutes. Fred W. Racoe, acting third assistant engineer, testified that "in about 2 minutes the fireroom was full of water and the fires all out in the furnace. But it was only one half a minute from the time of the explosion that the fires were extinguished and the engine stopped." The *Harvest Moon* was dead in the water.

There was widespread panic after the explosion, and Dahlgren noted:

> *Frightened men were struggling to lower the boats. I got by them with difficulty. They heard nothing; saw nothing. Passing from the gangway to the upper deck ladder, the open space was strewed with fragments of partitions. My foot went into some glass. The Fleet Captain was rushing down, and storming about. I ascended the ladder to get out on the upper deck to have a full view of things. A torpedo had been struck by poor old* Harvest Moon *and she was sinking.*

Fortunately, there were several Federal ships nearby, including the *Clover* and the *Pawnee*, and the men were evacuated quickly, as even Dahlgren realized that "there was no help for it, so we prepared to leave the vessel." Unbelievably, there was only one casualty: wardroom steward John Hazard, whose body was found the next day. Perhaps what contributed to the low casualty count, the rapidity with which the ship sank and the success with which the Federals salvaged everything usable from the ship was that it went down in two and a half fathoms of water—a depth of about fifteen feet. As a result, Crosby noted that even after it came to rest on the bottom, "the spar and hurricane deck was above water, and the gun deck [was just] one foot under water."

The USS *Pawnee. U.S. Navy Historical Center illustration.*

Immediately, the other Federal ships sent boats out to drag the area for torpedoes, but none was ever found. It was as if the hapless and unlucky *Harvest Moon* had hit the one remaining torpedo in all of Winyah Bay. The other Union ships posted an armed guard on the wreck—easy to do since its uppermost decks were above water—to keep any lingering Confederates from attempting to salvage anything usable from the ship. Over the next few days, the Federals had "all hands employed in unrigging ship unbinding sails…Engineers and Firemen employed in removing the machinery from the ship." The crew also removed any stores it could, even beef and pork stored in the hold. After removing the chains, anchors and every piece of usable machinery, on April 21, 1865, the Federals officially abandoned the wreck. By that time, the war was over, and though just a few weeks earlier efforts may have been made to raise the ship as it was in such shallow water, it was allowed to remain there, where it rests to this day.

A subsequent board of inquiry returned a verdict of "sunk by torpedo, no blame," noting:

> *There being no more required evidence the court, after due consideration,*
> *report the following facts: That the USS* Harvest Moon, *having the*

flag of Rear Admiral John Dahlgren was accidentally sunk by a torpedo placed in the Marsh Channel, Winyah Bay, South Carolina, on the first day of March 1865. That we fully and entirely exculpate from blame all on board said vessel at the time of the catastrophe there being no possible chance under the circumstances shown in the testimony of saving the vessel or preventing her from sinking.

At the end, the *Harvest Moon* had the distinction of being the only Union flagship sunk during the Civil War—another first for Captain Crosby and one he would live with for the rest of his days. To this day, the *Harvest Moon* sits in Winyah Bay, its rusted boiler visible as a mute testimony to an unlucky ship.

The Harvest Moon Today

Had the *Harvest Moon* gone down earlier in the war, no doubt it would have been salvaged and would have seen service once again, but by the time it was stripped and the Federals were ready to begin any operation to raise it, the war was over. Reconstruction became the focus of the Federal occupying forces in and around Georgetown. Thus, the *Harvest Moon* rested forgotten on the bottom in Winyah Bay. During the late nineteenth century, it must have been a majestic sight as its decks protruded above the water. No doubt, fishermen and all manner of boaters must have walked its decks and combed the wreck in search of souvenirs.

In time, however, the ship settled farther down into the alluvial mud of the bay, and storms—including a number of major hurricanes—and

A close-up of the boiler stack of the *Harvest Moon* as seen today. *Photograph courtesy of Scott Lawrence.*

sea raised the level of the mud as well. By the mid-1960s, roughly one hundred years after its sinking, it was estimated that perhaps six feet of mud covered the ship's top decks. Only its boiler stack still remained visible above the water.

In the 1960s, several enterprising groups and individuals began to show an interest in the *Harvest Moon*. In 1963, an expedition from the New England Naval and Maritime Museum began examining the wreck and determined that, at that time, the vessel was in extremely good condition. Another group called the Southern Explorations Association reportedly considered raising the *Harvest Moon* as a tourist attraction to serve in conjunction with a planned maritime museum on Front Street. There was a call for investors and apparently even talk of putting a World War II submarine periscope in the museum that afforded a view of the bay, but eventually this idea fell through as well. All this time, however, the *Harvest Moon* was officially a U.S. Navy ship, and only in February 1963 did Assistant Secretary of the Navy Kenneth E. BeLieu sign the document that granted the ship its release from the navy, allowing interested parties to salvage it if they desired. To date, that still hasn't happened, and salvage operations become less likely with each passing year.

This official U.S. Navy photo shows divers examining the *Harvest Moon* in 1963. *U.S. Navy Historical Center photograph.*

Today, the *Harvest Moon* rests approximately midway between Frazier's Point and the three marsh islands to the southeast, as seen on this *Mill's Atlas* map of Winyah Bay, circa 1825.

The Civil War from Georgetown to Little River

The *Harvest Moon*'s boiler stack in 2009. *Photograph courtesy of Scott Lawrence.*

Even today, all one needs is a boat with a very shallow draft (nautical charts mark the depth of the water around the boiler of the *Harvest Moon* at one to four feet), the right tide and a spirit of adventure, and you can take a trip out into Winyah Bay and touch the old boiler sticking up out of the water, all that remains of a once-great, if unlucky, ship.

A Timeline for Civil War–related Events from Georgetown to Little River

The following timeline includes the major incidents that occurred during the Civil War in the Horry-Georgetown district. Significant national events relating to the war are listed in boldface.

1860

December 20, 1860: South Carolina secedes from the Union.

1861

February 9, 1861: The Confederate States of America are formed.

February 27, 1861: Arthur Middleton Manigault tenders his services to the State of South Carolina as captain of the North Santee Mounted Rifles.

April 1861: Fort Randall is officially dedicated at Little River.

April 12, 1861: Confederates under General P.G.T. Beauregard open fire on Fort Sumter in Charleston, and the Civil War begins.

April 13, 1861: Major William Capers White writes to the Confederate secretary of war to tell him that the thirty-three men and three officers from Captain J. Litchfield's All Saints Riflemen have been posted at Fort Randall in Little River, and twenty-six men and two officers of the Waccamaw Light Artillery, along with twenty men and two officers of the Wachesaw Riflemen, are now stationed at Fort Ward in Murrells Inlet.

April 19, 1861: President Lincoln issues a Proclamation of Blockade against Southern ports.

August 1861: Colonel Arthur Middleton Manigault hears a report that Union troops have landed near Pawleys Island. Manigualt takes the CSS *Nina* and, with two companies of infantry, as well as the Georgetown Artillery under Captain James G. Henning, proceeds up to Hagley Plantation on the Waccamaw River. The Union landing turns out to be a false alarm.

August 9, 1861: Colonel Manigault takes a detachment of men onboard the *Nina* and captures a Union ship, and another Union ship sinks off of Georgetown in a storm.

November 1861: Federals invade and capture Hilton Head. Robert E. Lee is placed in command of the Department of South Carolina, Georgia and East Florida. Colonel Manigault (later to be promoted to brigadier general) of the Tenth Regiment, South Carolina Volunteers, was named commander of what was then known as the First Military District, which encompassed the defenses from the North Carolina line to the South Santee River. He will write to Lee on November 15, promising, "I will do the best I can should the enemy appear."

November 2, 1861: The Union steamer USS *Osceola* founders off of Georgetown, and two boats of crewmen are taken captive and sent to North Island and then on to Charleston.

A Timeline for Civil War–related Events

December 1861: With the threat of invasion in Georgetown less likely now that the Federals hold Hilton Head, troops in the Georgetown to Little River district are reduced to one thousand men.

December 13, 1861: Lieutenant George W. Browne of the USS *Fernandina* reports that he witnessed what he believed to be more than forty signal fires along the coast at Little River, which he judged were guides for a blockade runner or runners attempting to come in. Based on the number of men he saw when he ran in closer to shore, he realized that "there was an encampment of Confederate troops and the distant fires were their picket guard."

December 24, 1861: Chased and fired on by the USS *Gem of the Sea*, the blockade runner *Prince of Wales* grounds while attempting to run in at North Inlet. Union seamen try to tow it off as a prize, but a company of Confederate cavalry, led by Captain John H. Tucker, and a Confederate patrol, led by Lieutenant R.Z. Harllee, from Company D of the Tenth South Carolina Regiment, open fire. The Federals claim that the Confederate shots rain down "as fast as the scoundrels could fire their pieces." The Federals relinquish their prize.

1862

February 14, 1862: The *Gem of the Sea* sights a schooner trying to run in at Georgetown, and though the *Gem* fires on it and chases it for three hours, the schooner escapes.

February 27, 1862: The *Gem of the Sea* sights the schooner *British Queen* trying to run into Georgetown, and though the *Gem* loses it in the darkness, it will be captured off of Wilmington by the USS *Mount Vernon* the next day.

March 12, 1862: The *Gem of the Sea* captures the British blockade runner *Fair Play* off of Georgetown. The *Fair Play* will be armed with four twelve-pound howitzers and converted to a Federal ship of war later that year.

March 14, 1862: General John C. Pemberton is placed in overall command of the district.

March 20–27, 1862: The Confederate steamer CSS *Nashville*, the first ship to fly the Confederate flag in England when it arrived in Southampton in October 1861, is in Georgetown. On October 27, the commander of the USS *Keystone State* will learn that he has just missed it.

March 25, 1862: Pemberton writes Colonel Manigault, stating, "Having maturely considered the subject, I have determined to withdraw the forces from Georgetown, and therefore to abandon the position. You will proceed with all the infantry force under your command to this city, Charleston, and report to Brigadier General Ripley."

March 28, 1862: Manigault's troops leave for Charleston, and 903 men arrive in Mount Pleasant on April 3.

April 3, 1862: The USS *Keystone State* chases the runner *Seabrook* as it is coming out from Georgetown, and though it runs into the Santee to avoid capture, it is bottomed and crippled there.

April 10, 1862: The 180-ton schooner *Liverpool* tries to run into Georgetown, and as the *Keystone State* chases it, the *Liverpool* runs aground. Its crew burns it to prevent capture. Colonel Robert F. Graham of the Twenty-first South Carolina, who had remained in command of Georgetown after the transfer of Manigault and his men, is also ordered out of Georgetown. Command of the district now passes to Confederate Major William P. Emanuel.

April 15, 1862: The *Keystone State* and the *Gem of the Sea* chase a suspicious ship that proves to be the blockade runner *Success*. Though the ship flies the British flag, Commander William Le Roy of the *Keystone State* knows it to be "the former privateer *Dixie*, lately the *Kate Hale*, and now the *Success*." The ship is seized along with its cargo of "100 bales of cotton, 234 barrels spirits turpentine, 40 bushels peanuts, and 3000 pounds rice."

A Timeline for Civil War–related Events

April 25, 1862: Commander Le Roy of the *Keystone State* writes to Union Admiral Samuel F. DuPont and notes "the importance of Georgetown as a place for receiving and distributing supplies for the rebel states." He asks for "more vessels to blockade its waters."

May 21, 1862: The USS *Albatross* and the USS *Norwich* enter Winyah Bay and note that the Confederate forts on North, South and Cat Islands are deserted and armed only with Quaker guns.

May 22, 1862: The *Albatross* and the *Norwich* steam into Georgetown. Confederate Major William P. Emanuel has his men set fire to the turpentine-laden brig *Joseph* and set it adrift to block the Union ships, but to no effect. Later that afternoon, the two Union ships go up the Waccamaw River and raid a mill, carrying off eighty slaves in the process.

May 26, 1862: The blockade runners *Lucy Holmes*, *Emma* and *Caroline* all run out of the Santee successfully.

May 31, 1862: Union General Daniel Hunter thinks that the Georgetown area should be a high-priority target, noting that "there is said to be 4,000,000 or 5,000,000 bushels [of rice there]. It is important that we should have this rice, and that the enemy should be deprived of it."

June 1, 1862: General Robert E. Lee assumes command of the Confederate Army of Northern Virginia.

June 3, 1862: The *Gem of the Sea* captures the blockade runner *Mary Stewart*.

June 5, 1862: The *Gem of the Sea* goes up the South Santee and picks up five contrabands from Blake's Plantation.

June 20, 1862: Federals in the *Albatross* capture the blockade runner *Louisa* and the tug *Treaty* near Georgetown. The schooner *Louisa* is captured on the Santee loaded with 147 bales of cotton and two lighters of rice. The tug *Treaty* is captured off the Georgetown bar and will eventually be sheathed with two-inch planks and armed with a rifled howitzer for use against the Confederates.

June 24, 1862: A Federal expedition consisting of the *Albatross* and the steamers USS *Western World*, USS *E.B. Hale* and USS *Henry Andrew*, as well as the steam tug *North Santee*, head up the South Santee River, intent on destroying the Northeastern Railroad bridge. Several ships run aground.

June 25, 1862: It becomes obvious that only the *E.B. Hale* can actually make it upriver, so the mission that began on the twenty-fourth is aborted. On the way back downriver, the ships are fired upon by Confederate "artillery, riflemen, and cavalry" according to Commander George Prentiss. Union marines burn Blake's Plantation and destroy a large supply of rice. Union soldiers plunder the plantation, prompting a rebuke from Secretary of the Navy Gideon Welles. On the northern end of the coast, boats from the USS *Penobscot*, the USS *Mystic*, the USS *Mount Vernon*, the USS *Victoria* and two from the USS *Monticello* enter Little River inlet to destroy blockade runners reported to be there. The Federals destroy two schooners, sixty bales of cotton, two hundred barrels of turpentine and fifty-three barrels of rosin.

June 30, 1862: Federal ships ascend the Waccamaw River in order to secure five lighters of rice to feed the growing contrabands colony on North Island.

July 2, 1862: The USS *Western World* captures the British runner *Volante* in Winyah Bay. It carries a cargo of salt and fish. Other Confederate ships and runners in the area at the time include the *Nina*; the *Weenee*, a 50-ton side-wheel steamer; the *Orah Peck*, a 150-ton schooner; and the *General Ripley*, a 175-ton side-wheel steamer.

July 3, 1862: Federal Naval Commander George Prentiss declares attempts to ascend the South Santee River a "failure" and orders the *E.B. Hale* and the *Henry Andrew* out of the area.

July 5, 1862: In light of recent Union incursions in the Georgetown area, Adjutant and Inspector General Samuel Cooper suggests to General Pemberton that "it would be well to occupy…Georgetown, constructing the necessary works, and placing…a garrison of the best artillery sufficient to serve the requisite number of guns, so as to prevent the entrance of marauding vessels." Pemberton replies, "We cannot protect the whole coast. If it is attempted to put guns in position at…Georgetown they will be lost."

July 10, 1862: Pressed again by Cooper to fortify Georgetown, Pemberton argues, "It is absolutely impossible to put guns on…South or Cat Islands, near Georgetown. The enemy's gunboats can always prevent it; they command those places." On July 11, Pemberton again argues, "No more troops can be spared for the defense of Georgetown and vicinity. Heavy guns for that purpose are out of the question."

July 21, 1862: The *Western World*, the *Gem of the Sea* and the *Treaty* steam into Murrells Inlet, and while a Federal landing party is demolishing saltworks, they are attacked by twenty-five Confederates. Though under fire, the Federals destroy the saltworks, scattering the salt among the sand at a cost of only two Federal wounded.

July 29, 1862: The USS *Pocahontas* goes up the Waccamaw River, taking on twenty-eight contrabands at Dr. Joseph Magill's plantation.

August 1862: Acting on a request from Confederate secretary of the navy Stephen R. Mallory, Annapolis graduate Lieutenant Alphonse Barbot recommends Mars Bluff, South Carolina, as the site for a Confederate navy yard.

August 3, 1862: Deferring to higher authorities at last, General Pemberton visits Georgetown to select locations on which to build new forts to defend Georgetown and block access to all of the area's rivers. He selects Mayrant's Bluff and Frazier's Point on Winyah Bay for the sites of the new forts.

August 7, 1862: As a stop-gap measure until the forts on Winyah Bay are completed, Confederate troops reoccupy the fort at Laurel Hill with a force of 150 men, and new earthworks up the Black River are garrisoned as well.

August 8, 1862: Alarmed by the July attacks by the Federals on the LaBruce and Ward saltworks in Murrells Inlet, Peter Vaught writes to Columbia to ask for state troops to guard property and saltworks he owns in what is now Myrtle Beach.

August 14, 1862: The *Pocahontas* and the *Treaty* set out in search of the *Nina*, the Waccamaw Light Artillery and any fortifications that they can destroy. Confederate batteries at Sparkman's Plantation open fire. Commander Balch of the *Pocahontas* notes, "The bluffs were lined with troops, and for a distance of 20 miles we had to run the gauntlet." Major Emanuel claims, "I don't think the enemy's loss could have been less than 50 killed and wounded."

August 29, 1862: General Pemberton is relieved of command of the district and transferred, and Confederate General P.G.T. Beauregard is given command of the Department of South Carolina, Georgia and East Florida.

September 17, 1862: Major William Capers White, who was one of the first officers to organize the defenses along the coast, is killed at Sharpsburg.

October 1862: Beauregard selects a local man, Brigadier General James Heyward Trapier, to command the troops in the Georgetown area. Confederate Charles Ost laments the lack of safe ports between Georgetown and Cape Fear. Major A.B. Magruder suggests Little River, as it "is not down on the charts nor on the coast survey, and its existence even—certainly its harbor and anchorage ground—is hardly known to any Yankee."

October 8, 1862: Beauregard writes to Governor Francis Pickens and assures him that he has given orders for the construction of a battery of five or six pieces of artillery for the defense of Winyah Bay.

November 10, 1862: General Beauregard writes to Colonel James Chestnut in Columbia and orders a regiment of state troops to Trapier's position to man the "batteries until other forces can be sent in that direction."

Beauregard sends an engineer to examine the Santee in order to find sites for underwater obstructions, to fortify a battery at Nowell's Point and to construct a new battery on the North Santee at Ladson's Bluff.

November 11, 1862: Two Federal gunboats steam into Winyah Bay and start firing on the fort at Mayrant's Bluff. They are met by returning fire from the Second South Carolina Artillery under the command of Captain Frederick F. Warley. After a few minutes, the Federals retire.

November 17, 1862: Trapier is appalled at the state militia he has been sent, noting that they "arrived without arms and without ammunition…It is questionable whether they can be rendered efficient…even if well armed and equipped. At present they are literally worth nothing at all."

November 21, 1862: Federal naval commander J.C. Beaumont of the USS *Sebago* notes that construction is under way at Mayrant's Bluff.

November 24, 1862: The USS *Monticello* bombards and destroys two extensive saltworks near Little River Inlet.

December 16, 1862: Secretary Mallory writes to Lieutenant William G. Dozier, who is in charge of operations at the Mars Bluff navy yard, and notifies him that "the department relies on you to complete [your work], in the shortest possible time…push the work on night and day."

December 24, 1862: Secretary Mallory writes to Lieutenant Dozier once again, telling him that "a paymaster and constructor are on the way to Mars Bluff to report to you." A large detail of men, including Acting Naval Constructor John L. Porter, CSN, shipwrights and the support staff the navy yard needs, are soon on site, and the work begins.

December 30, 1862: Runaway slaves taken aboard the USS *Victoria* inform the Federals that two blockade runners, the *Argyle* and the *James Bailey*, are anchored at Little River and are ready to run out.

December 31, 1862: A reconnaissance party from the *Victoria* attempts to land near Little River but encounters a patrol of Confederate cavalry from Fort Randall and is forced to withdraw. The Federals proceed upriver and attempt another landing but again stumble on Confederate pickets.

1863

January 1, 1863: President Lincoln issues the Emancipation Proclamation, freeing all slaves in territories held by Confederates.

January 2, 1863: The *Victoria* captures the schooner *Argyle*, although the runner *James Bailey* is able to slip away in the confusion and run out.

January 5, 1863: Twenty-five men led by Lieutenant William Barksdale Cushing briefly capture Fort Randall until they are driven out by Confederate troops.

January 11, 1863: The schooner *Florida* is captured near Little River.

January 15, 1863: The *Lotus*, a ship out of Boston carrying supplies for the Federal troops stationed at Port Royal, runs ashore on North Island. Commander Beaumont of the USS *Sebago* notes that when his men attempt to remove the cargo, they are surprised to find liquor hidden among the supplies. Most of the cargo is lost.

February 1863: Battery White at Mayrant's Bluff is complete.

February 3, 1863: General Trapier reports that Captain Warley has fifty-three men at Battery White manning nine guns. The Waccamaw Light Artillery is stationed at Frazier's Point with fieldpieces.

February 9, 1863: Reconnaissance boats from the USS *Maratanza* capture a Confederate supply boat, five soldiers and supplies heading for Fort Randall. They learn that there is one company of cavalry and one company of infantry stationed at Fort Randall, totaling 175 men in all.

A Timeline for Civil War–related Events

February 22, 1863: The *Matthew Vassar* and the *Victoria* report barely missing a steamer running out of Little River. Later that night, a runner trying to enter the inlet sees the two Union ships on blockading duty and returns to the high seas.

February 24, 1863: A steamer trying to run into Little River comes upon a patrolling Federal guard boat from the *Matthew Vassar* but escapes when the Federals try to board it.

February 24, 1863: The English blockade runner *Queen of the Wave* runs aground in the North Santee River and is set afire by its captain to keep it from being captured. On the morning of the twenty-fifth, the ship is still visible and unburned, so sailors from the USS *Conemaugh* set out to destroy it. The *Conemaugh's* men discover onboard seven Confederate soldiers of the Waccamaw Light Artillery who had been conducting salvage operations all night. The Confederates surrender, and are taken onboard the USS *Quaker City*. The *Queen of the Wave* is blown up.

March 1863: The allotment of troops in the district area is 336 cavalry and 142 artillerymen, a total of 478 men.

March 3, 1863: The *Matthew Vassar* sends Acting Master's Mate George Drain and a party of seven men to destroy a boat beached near Little River, but Confederate troops from Fort Randall capture them. Captain Benjamin F. Sands of the USS *Dacotah* is so incensed at the capture of Drain and the men from the *Matthew Vassar*—under circumstances "so unaccountable…that it looks to me very like a desertion, or at best an act of recklessness without apparent object, and a great want of ordinary prudence and caution"—that he orders the *Matthew Vassar* relieved of duty in the area.

March 7, 1863: The USS *Victoria* reports "a large number of men in [Fort Randall]…with a large flag flying and much cheering." The *Victoria* shells the fort, forcing the Confederates out, and picks up a member of the *Vassar's* crew who had escaped capture on the third and had been hiding since.

March 21, 1863: The *Victoria* and the *William Bacon* sight a steamer trying to run into Little River and open fire on it. It proves to be the *Nicolai I*, a blockade runner out of Nassau.

March 30, 1863: The USS *Monticello* captures the steamer *Sue* off of Little River. The *Sue* has apparently recently unloaded salt somewhere between Georgetown and Little River.

April 20–21, 1863: Commander A.K. Hughes of the USS *Cimarron* sends a party of thirty armed men to destroy a mill upriver below Georgetown.

April 25, 1863: While chasing a blockade runner, Lieutenant Commander D.L. Braine of the USS *Monticello* notes that in Murrells Inlet "there are five large schooners and large buildings, evidently storehouses." He writes to his superior, Captain Charles S. Boggs, "With your permission, I can easily destroy them in a day, and I would like to do so, if it meets with your approval." Boggs tells Braine, "I hope you can clear out this nest…if successful, run no risk in bringing out prizes, but destroy them."

April 27, 1863: The *Monticello* and the *Matthew Vassar* appear at Murrells Inlet and shell the inlet for more than two hours. The Federals send out boats and destroy the schooner *Golden Liner*, along with two storehouses nearby. The Federals learn that more than two hundred Confederate infantry and cavalry are approaching, and they return to their ships. One Federal sailor is wounded and another is captured in the retreat. The *Monticello* and the *Matthew Vassar* resume their bombardment of the inlet, which continues until the ships withdraw later that afternoon.

April 29, 1863: After the attack on Murrells Inlet on the twenty-seventh, Confederate Lieutenant Colonel Joseph Yates calls up a section of artillery from Georgetown for Murrells Inlet and orders Captain Boykin to bring down his troops from Fort Randall. "They are not aware of present force at that point," he writes, "and will no doubt make another effort [to attack]."

A Timeline for Civil War–related Events

May 3, 1863: The USS *Maratanza* and the USS *Chocura* anchor off of Murrells Inlet and begin shelling. The Federals send ashore a boat, and Major Emanuel's Fourth South Carolina Cavalry opens fire, killing one Federal sailor and seriously wounding three others. After this failure, Commander G.H. Scott of the *Maratanza* cautiously notes that he is "convinced from the rebel forces at this place of the utter impracticability of attempting a boat expedition for the destruction of the vessels, as the route is long, circuitous, and protected for a great distance by thickly wooded banks, affording the best possible cover for the large number of infantry now collected here."

May 8–9, 1863: The Fourth South Carolina Cavalry leaves the district on the ninth, having been replaced by two companies of the Twenty-first Battalion Georgia Cavalry on the eighth. In addition to the Georgia troops, in Murrells Inlet and Georgetown there is a company of cavalry under Captain John H. Tucker, Captain Ward's Waccamaw Artillery and Company D of the Second South Carolina Artillery under Lieutenant William E. Charles. Lieutenant Colonel Yates, however, is told that Murrells Inlet is "not regarded as of great military importance," though the Federals appear to believe otherwise. On May 8, Rear Admiral Samuel DuPont orders the USS *Conemaugh* and the USS *Flambeau* to Murrells Inlet to "establish a blockade off that entrance."

May 11, 1863: The *Conemaugh* and the *Monticello* anchor about two thousand yards off of Murrells Inlet and begin shelling. The Federals do not attempt a landing, however, as Commander Reed Werden of the *Conemaugh* reports though that "the inlet [is] too narrow for [his ship] to enter" and that "the enemy have increased their force, having now artillery, cavalry, and infantry." In two and a half hours, his ship alone fires more than one hundred rounds of ammunition, and the Federal bombardment damages five ships in the inlet. One, the *Golden Liner*, is completely destroyed.

June 23, 1863: The *Flambeau* captures the blockade runner *Bettie Cratzer* off of Murrells Inlet.

July 1–3, 1863: The Battle of Gettysburg is a major Confederate defeat.

July 4, 1863: General John Pemberton, now in command of Vicksburg, surrenders thirty thousand Confederate troops to Ulysses S. Grant. It will be the last assignment Pemberton will ever have as a general.

October 16, 1863: Rear Admiral John A. Dahlgren, now commanding the South Atlantic Blockading Squadron, writes to Master W.L. Babcock of the USS *T.A. Ward* and orders Babcock to Murrells Inlet "for the purpose of observing a strict blockade of the place."

October 17, 1863: The blockade runner *Rover* attempts to run into Murrells Inlet and is driven ashore. The *Rover*'s crew removes its cargo to a spot behind the sand dunes and burns the ship.

October 20, 1863: In Murrells Inlet, after the *T.A. Ward* shells "a large frame building, where it supposed Rebel cavalry were concealed," two boats go ashore. They are surprised by Confederate cavalry, and one Federal is killed and the others are captured.

November 4, 1863: Admiral Dahlgren writes to Secretary of the Navy Gideon Welles and notes that the Confederates are using Murrells Inlet because the blockade of Charleston "is driving speculators to the smaller ports." "I shall dispatch a gunboat to stop that game," Dahlgren writes.

November 5, 1863: Four Federal ships—the USS *Fulton*, the USS *Nansemond*, the USS *Howquah* and the USS *Keystone State* –are sent after and capture the notorious blockade runner *Margaret and Jessie* off of what is now Myrtle Beach.

November 6, 1863: Admiral Dahlgren sends the gunboat USS *Ottawa* to the blockade at Murrells Inlet.

A Timeline for Civil War–related Events

November 14, 1863: The schooner *George Chisolm* runs out of Georgetown with a cargo of salt and is overtaken and captured near the South Santee by the USS *Dai Ching*.

November 30, 1863: At Mars Bluff, the CSS *Pee Dee* is reported to be "advancing to completion" and its "machinery is ready."

December 5, 1863: In what will become the most controversial event in the district during the war, the USS *Perry* lands two boats below Murrells Inlet. Confederate cavalry bear down on them and force their retreat, and another company of cavalry take the boats, forcing their surrender. One Federal prisoner is shot and killed, and George Brimsmaid, a black freedman, will apparently be marched off and hanged. The final toll is four Federal dead, and the Confederates have one man killed and another two wounded. Disgusted by this latest debacle, Dahlgren says, "It was a blundering affair, without judgment on the part of the commanding officer, and aggravated by the alleged disobedience of the officer sent ashore in charge of the party."

December 23, 1863: Admiral Dahlgren, angered by repeated Union failures in Murrells Inlet, writes, "I desire…to administer some corrective to the small parties of rebels who infest that vicinity, and shall detail for that purpose the *Nipsic, Sanford, Geranium*, and *Daffodil*, and also the sailing bark [*Ethan*] *Allen* and the schooner *Mangham*, 100 Marines for landing, and four howitzers, two for boats, two on field carriages, with such boats as may be needed."

December 29, 1863: The USS *Nipsic*, the USS *Sanford*, the USS *Daffodil* and the USS *Ethan Allen*, with a landing force of 250 men, set out for Murrells Inlet, and on the thirtieth, they are joined by the USS *George Mangham*. A storm disperses the ships before the attack can commence.

1864

January 1864: There are now eleven pieces of artillery in Battery White, though none of the guns is large enough to repel ironclads.

January 1, 1864: The *Nipsic* returns to bombard Murrells Inlet and to destroy a schooner. Forty men in two cutters with thirty marines open fire on the schooner, and Admiral Dahlgren reported "she took fire and, with a valuable cargo of turpentine, was soon in one blaze." These men returned to the *Nipsic* without mishap.

January 7, 1864: The blockade runner *Dare* is run aground north of Georgetown at North Inlet by the USS *Aries* and the USS *Montgomery*. The Federals attempt to land a shore party to salvage the ship, but the barges capsize and three seamen drown. The survivors are captured by Major William P. White, commander of the Twenty-first Georgia Cavalry, and Second Lieutenant Thomas Young and Private Lemuel Robertson, both of Company C of White's regiment, without firing a shot.

January 12, 1864: The *Aries* leaves the blockade runner *Vesta* "a complete wreck, with five feet of water in her" at Little River.

January 19, 1864: Confederate pickets report three Union ships patrolling just below Battery White.

February 1, 1864: General Trapier notes the desertions of the Third and Fourth South Carolina state troops, under the command of Lieutenant Colonel R.A. Rouse and Colonel J.H. Witherspoon.

February 17, 1864: Trapier writes to Beauregard, lamenting conditions in the district and noting that he now has only about three hundred men in his command. He argues that unless he is given more troops, "the navy yard at Mars Bluff [will] be exposed to almost certain destruction. For even supposing [Union] boats should not be able to navigate the river so high up, a few hundred cavalry, landed on its banks 20 or 30 miles below, could by a sudden dash complete the work of destruction in a very few hours."

February 17, 1864: The CSS *Hunley* rams the USS *Housatonic* using a torpedo attached to a spar, and the *Housatonic* goes down in minutes. The *Housatonic*'s captain, J.K. Crosby, will next be the captain of the USS *Harvest Moon*.

A Timeline for Civil War–related Events

March 1864: The two companies of the Twenty-first Georgia Cavalry that have been stationed in Murrells Inlet and Company D of the Second South Carolina Artillery are transferred out of the district; they will eventually be replaced by Company B of the German Artillery.

March 1, 1864: Off of Little River, the USS *Connecticut* captures the blockade runner *Scotia*, a side-wheel steamer out of Glasgow laden with 220 bales of cotton.

March 2, 1864: The Union navy lands troops below Battery White and pushes back the Confederate pickets, though no further action ensues.

March 8, 1864: Trapier reports that Battery White is "well-constructed and of ample dimensions" but "feebly armed."

March 18, 1864: Captain Tucker's company of independent cavalry is made Company F of the regular Seventh South Carolina Cavalry and sent to Virginia.

April 15, 1864: The Federals station two more ships, the USS *Ethan Allen* and the USS *Cimarron*, in the Georgetown area in order to shut down the blockade-running traffic.

April 16, 1864: Robert Blake, one of the contrabands sent to North Island after the Union raid up the Santee on June 24, 1862, wins the Congressional Medal of Honor for bravery while serving on the USS *Marblehead*. He is just the second African American to be so designated and the first to actually receive the medal.

April 21, 1864: The *Cimarron* slips up the Santee River and destroys a rice mill and five thousand bushels of rice. The *Ethan Allen* sets out from Murrells Inlet, heads up the coast and destroys Peter Vaught's saltworks. The works include three warehouses, one of which was a Confederate blockhouse, and mount forty-eight salt pans, with twelve more standing ready to be mounted.

April 22, 1864: The *Ethan Allen* destroys another saltworks at Withers Swash.

April 30, 1864: Confederate naval Lieutenant Oscar Johnson, a graduate of the United States Naval Academy, is sent to Mars Bluff with a contingent of ninety men and officers to assume command of the *Pee Dee* when it is ready to be launched.

May 1864: The armament at Battery White consists of a thirty-two-pound smoothbore, one twelve-pound smoothbore, six twenty-four-pound smoothbores, one six-pound smoothbore, three thirty-two-pound rifles, three twelve-pound rifles and one three-and-a-half-inch Blakely. The Waccamaw Light Artillery had three six-pounders and one three-and-a-half-inch Blakely at the unfinished earthworks and trenches on Frazier's Point.

May 14, 1864: Admiral Dahlgren writes that he and General John Porter Hatch, who had more than fourteen thousand men in his command, are planning "an incursion…into the country between Georgetown and Murrells Inlet." However, Hatch is relieved of command and the plans are cancelled.

June 2, 1864: The USS *Wamsutta* chases the side-wheel steamer *Rose* to ground on North Island. As soon as the *Rose* sees the *Wamsutta* approaching, she runs for the south end of Pawleys Island but accidentally "runs ashore near the wreck of another steamer and some buildings on the beach." The *Wamsutta* sends a boat to save the vessel as a prize, but seventy-five Confederate cavalrymen come from the north end of Pawleys Island and open fire on the Federals, forcing them to abandon the project.

September 1864: Captain Thomas West Daggett and Lieutenant Stephen A. Rouquie construct mines on the second floor of a store owned by the Rouquies on Front Street in Georgetown. Daggett has the mines laid at strategic intervals in Winyah Bay, ready to detonate if struck by an invading Federal warship. One of their mines will sink the *Harvest Moon* in March 1865.

A Timeline for Civil War–related Events

October 5, 1864: Eleven privates from Company B of the German Artillery desert to the USS *Potomska*. The Federals learn that "at Battery White there are ten guns…in the rear of the battery there is a section of artillery consisting of two rifled 12-pounders."

October 29, 1864: Admiral John Dahlgren writes to Commander N.B. Harrison on the USS *Canandaigua*, "I have been informed that the Rebels have built a Gunboat on the 'Peedee,' which may be expected to come down as soon as the river is high enough. She is said to be of light draft, and to carry eight guns, of which two are ten inch. The account may be exaggerated but it is well to be prepared."

November 15, 1864: General Sherman, with sixty-two thousand men, begins his March to the Sea.

November 19, 1864: General Trapier, who has only 361 men and twenty-two officers in the district, loses Kirk's Rangers and Gaillard's Artillery.

December 21, 1864: General Sherman reaches Savannah, leaving a three-hundred-mile swath of destruction in his wake, all the way from Atlanta.

December 22, 1864: Off of Savannah, the *Harvest Moon* becomes grounded in the mud and is unable to be moved until the following day. General William T. Sherman is aboard for a council of war, and having left orders for his army to stay put in his absence, General William Hardee's Confederates are able to evacuate Savannah that same night. Sherman writes on January 1, 1865, to Chief of Staff General Henry Halleck, lamenting the fact that he is "very much disappointed" as a result.

1865

January 1865: General Trapier and all soldiers except the German Artillery are ordered out of the district. By the end of the month, the highest-ranking officer left in the district is Lieutenant Hermann

Klatte, who has been ordered to hold out for as long as possible and then withdraw.

February 5, 1865: Lieutenant William B. Cushing takes fifty men in four boats from the USS *Monticello* and captures Little River. His men destroy an estimated $15,000 worth of cotton on the docks there.

February 17, 1865: Charleston, South Carolina falls.

February 20, 1865: Lieutenant Klatte and the German Artillery finally evacuate Battery White, and the people of Georgetown are left to their own devices.

February 25, 1865: Georgetown surrenders and the town is occupied by six companies of Federal marines.

February 26, 1865: The CSS *Pee Dee* completes its only mission successfully by covering the retreat of General Hardee's troops as they cross the Pee Dee River at Cheraw.

February 26, 1865: Admiral John Dahlgren arrives in Georgetown and declares martial law.

February 28, 1865: Admiral Dahlgren inspects Battery White, noting, "Generally it has been much underrated…but we can now understand it was well placed, well constructed, and strongly armed, so we should have had some trouble to reduce it if well manned."

March 1865: Georgetown citizens meet with Captain H.S. Stellwagen of the *Pawnee* and ask for help. About thirty Confederate deserters have commandeered a flatboat and are raiding up and down the Waccamaw River, and Stellwagen orders the *Mingoe* upriver to search for the marauders. Later in March, another expedition is mounted to drive out the deserters, this time involving the *Mingoe*, the *Catalpa*, four large launches, ten boats and three hundred troops.

A Timeline for Civil War–related Events

March 1, 1865: Admiral Dahlgren orders the *Harvest Moon* to head back to Charleston. At about 7:45 a.m., the *Harvest Moon* strikes a "torpedo" and sinks in less than five minutes.

March 4–15, 1865: Lieutenant Oscar Johnson and his men burn the *Pee Dee* after all usable supplies and ammunition are unloaded. Lieutenant Johnson has the crew fire a single defiant shot into the woods.

April 9, 1865: General Lee surrenders to General Ulysses S. Grant at Appomattox Court House, Virginia.

April 18, 1865: Confederate General Joseph E. Johnston surrenders to Sherman near Durham in North Carolina. Though Confederate forces will continue to surrender for another month, essentially the war is over.

April 21, 1865: After the *Harvest Moon* is stripped of every usable piece of equipment, it is officially abandoned as a wreck.

BIBLIOGRAPHY

Anderson, Thom. "Dixie Gunboat Being Hauled to New Port." *Florence Morning News,* August 23, 1961.

Arthur Manigault Chapter of the United Daughters of the Confederacy. *For Love of a Rebel.* N.p., 1964.

Atlas to Accompany the Official Records of the Union and Confederate Armies. 3 vols. Washington D.C.: U.S. Government Printing Office, 1891–1895.

Baker, Gary R. *Cadets in Gray: The Story of the Cadets of the South Carolina Military Academy and the Cadet Rangers in the Civil War.* Columbia, SC: Palmetto Bookworks, 1989.

"Battery White." http://batterywhite.org (accessed April 2009).

Boatner, Mark Mayo, III. *The Civil War Dictionary.* New York: David McKay Company, 1959.

Chaitin, Peter M. *The Coastal War: Chesapeake Bay to Rio Grande.* Chicago: Time-Life Books, 1984.

Dabbs, James Mcbride. *Pee Dee Panorama.* Columbia: University of South Carolina Press, 1951.

Davis, William C., et al. *Brother Against Brother: The War Begins.* Chicago: Time-Life Books, 1983.

Department of the Navy. "Naval Historical Center." http://www.history. navy.mil/branches/nhcorg11.htm (accessed 2008–2009).

Donnelly, Ralph W. *The Confederate States Marine Corps: The Rebel Leathernecks.* N.p.: White Mane Publishing Company, 1989.

Drucker, Lesley M. *A Cultural Resources Inventory of Selected Areas of The Oaks and Laurel Hill Plantations, Brookgreen Gardens*. N.p.: Carolina Archeological Services, 1980.

Elting, Colonel John R., et al. *The Blockade: Runners and Raiders*. Chicago: Time-Life Books, 1983.

Evans, Clement A. *Confederate Military History: South Carolina*. Atlanta: Blue and Gray Press, 1899.

Gibbons, Tony. *Warships and Naval Battles of the Civil War*. New York: Gallery Books, 1989.

Gragg, Ted. E-mail message to the author on "CSS *Pee Dee*." August 1–3, 2008.

Harvest Moon Society. "Harvest Moon Society's Website." http://www.bjpeters.com /HarvestMoon/ (accessed 2008).

Horry County Historical Society. http://hchsonline.org/ (accessed 2008).

Horry Dispatch, May 9 1861.

Independent Republic Quarterly. Vols. 3, 4, 6, 9, 12, 14, 19 & 20. Conway, SC: Horry County Historical Society, 1967–present.

Johnson, Robert Underwood, and Clarence Clough Buel, eds. *Battles and Leaders of the Civil War*. 4 vols. Secaucus, NJ: Castle, 1983.

King, G. Wayne. *History of Florence County*. Spartanburg, SC: Reprint Company, 1981.

Linder, Suzanne, and Maria Thacker. *Historical Atlas of the Rice Plantations of Georgetown County and the Santee River*. N.p.: South Carolina Department of Archives and History, 2001.

Maritime Research Division. "Mars Bluff Confederate Navy Yard." http://www.cas.sc.edu/sciaa/mrd/scuaaprevlicprojs.html (accessed February 2008).

Michie, James L. *Richmond Hill Plantation, 1810–1868: The Discovery of Antebellum Life on a Waccamaw Rice Plantation*. Spartanburg, SC: Reprint Company, 1990.

National Register of Historic Places Nomination Form. "Battery White." South Carolina Department of Archives and History. http://www.nationalregister.sc.gov/georgetown/S10817722010/S10817722010.pdf (accessed August 2008).

Official Records of the Union and Confederate Navies in the War of the Rebellion. 30 vols. Washington, D.C.: U.S. Government Printing Office, 1894–1922.

"Pee Dee Gunboat: A Link with History." *Florence Morning News*, December 13, 1957.

Petit, James Percival, ed. *South Carolina and the Sea: Day by Day Toward Five Centuries, 1492–1985 A.D.* Vol. II. Isle of Palms, SC: Le Petit Maison Publishers, Ltd. 1986.

Quattlebaum, Laura Janette. *The History of Horry County, South Carolina.* N.p., n.d.

"Researchers Hunt Spanish Shipwreck." *Coastal Observer*, August 28, 2008.

Rogers, George C., Jr. *The History of Georgetown County, South Carolina.* Columbia: University of South Carolina Press, 1970.

———. *Theodosia and Other Pee Dee Sketches.* Columbia, SC: R.L. Bryan Company, 1978.

Roske, Ralph J., and Charles Van Doren. *Lincoln's Commando: The Biography of Commander William B. Cushing USN.* New York: Harper and Row, 1957.

Sloan, L.C. "Battery White, (1862–1865)." *Georgetown County Historic Register* (1971).

South Carolina Department of Archives and History. "Battery White, Georgetown County." http://www.nationalregister.sc.gov/georgetown/S10817722010/index.htm.

Still, William J. "Facilities for the Construction of War Vessels in the Confederacy." *Journal of Southern History* 31, no. 3 (August 1965): 285–304.

Tower, R. Lockwood. *A Carolinian Goes to War: The Civil War Narrative of Arthur Middleton Manigault.* Columbia: University of South Carolina Press, 1983.

Townsend, Leah. "The Confederate Gunboat Pedee." *South Carolina Historical and Genealogical Magazine* 60 (n.d.).

Warner, Ezra J. *Generals in Blue.* Baton Rouge: Louisiana State University Press, 1964.

———. *Generals in Gray.* Baton Rouge: Louisiana State University Press, 1964.

The War of the Rebellion: A Compilation of the Official Records of the Union and Confederate Armies. 128 vols. Washington, D.C.: U.S. Government Printing Office, 1880–1901.

INDEX

A

All Saints Riflemen 34, 156
Allston, Lieutenant L. Bacot 52
Amelia Island 108
Anderson, Ensign George 78, 79,
    80
Andersonville Prison 77, 79, 94
Annie 92
Argyle 36, 42, 163, 164
Arrants, Ensign William B. 95
Arrow. See Hero

B

Babcock, Master W.L 76, 168
Balch, Commander George 55,
    56, 58, 59, 91, 132, 162
Barbot, Lieutenant Alphonse 126,
    161
Barnes, Lieutenant Commander 133
Battery White 23, 35, 43, 47, 60,
    67, 69, 74, 103, 112–19,
    122, 124, 133, 144, 145,
    147, 164, 169, 170–74
Baxter, Commander I.B. 20, 50,
    51, 58, 69, 87, 91
Beaty, John R. 17, 23–25

Beaumont, Commander J.C. 93,
    109, 163, 164
Beauregard, General P.G.T. 13,
    23, 59, 60, 77, 107–10, 113,
    131, 155, 162, 163, 170
Benton, Lieutenant D.L. 89
Bettie Cratzer 75, 94, 167
Black River 11, 14, 48, 56, 58, 91,
    101, 103, 107, 161
Blake, Robert 54, 171
Blake's Plantation 50–52, 54, 91,
    159, 160
Boggs, Captain Charles S. 71, 166
Bonham, Governor Milledge 60
Bowen, Captain C.C. 78
Boykin, Captain A.H. 34, 38, 72,
    73, 166
Boykin, Captain Ed. 61
Bragg, General Braxton 108
Braine, Lieutenant Commander
    D.L. 69, 71, 73, 166
Breckinridge, John C. 146
Brimsmaid, George 78–80, 169
British Queen 88, 157
Brown, Acting Master L.A. 71
Browne, Lieutenant George W. 35,
    157

Bullis, Ensign W.H. 146
Bunting, Ensign James 62
Byrd, Major Stephen D 51

C

Camden Mounted Rifles 34, 38,
    72, 73
Camp Chestnut 13, 63
Camp Harlee 13, 63
Camp Lookout 13
Camp Magill 13, 56, 63
Camp Marion 13
Camp Middleton 13, 63
Camp Norman 13, 17
Camp Trapier 13, 63
Camp Waccamaw 13, 63, 68, 74
Carolina 99
Carolina Greys 34
Caroline 90
Cat Island 13, 14, 21, 23–25, 30,
    68, 103, 105, 107, 127
Cecilia 77, 78, 94
Chaplain, Lieutenant Commander
    James C. 95
Charles, Lieutenant William E. 74
Charleston, South Carolina 12,
    17, 19, 31, 32, 35, 48, 68,
    77, 87, 100, 103, 104, 108,
    109, 113, 117, 141–45, 155,
    156, 158, 168, 174, 175
Charlotte, North Carolina 135
Cheraw, South Carolina 134, 135,
    174
Clayton, Midshipman William F.
    135
Clements, Lieutenant L.L. 34
Colcock, Colonel John 134
Columbus, Georgia 127
Confederate Torpedo Bureau 146
Cooper, Inspector General Samuel
    55, 131, 160, 161

Creighton, Commander J. Blakely
    117, 132
Crosby, Master J.K. 143–46, 148,
    150, 171
CSS *Albemarle* 37
CSS *Hunley* 143, 144, 170
CSS *Macon* 135
CSS *Merrimac* 37, 144
CSS *Nashville* 88, 158
CSS *Nina* 56, 58, 85, 86, 91, 92,
    100, 128, 156, 160, 162
CSS *Pee Dee* 47, 99, 100, 101, 113,
    125, 128–36, 138, 139, 169,
    172, 174, 175
CSS *Sampson* 135
Cushing, Lieutenant William
    Barksdale 37, 38, 42, 44,
    45, 100, 164, 174, 179

D

Daggett, Captain Thomas West
    17, 34, 147, 172
Dahlgren, Admiral John A. 43,
    76–81, 99, 100, 115,
    117–19, 130, 132, 140–46,
    148, 150, 168–70, 172–75
Dare 96, 170
Department of Mississippi 107
Department of South Carolina,
    Georgia and East Florida
    156, 162
Department of South Carolina,
    Georgia and Florida 107
District of Eastern and Middle
    Florida 108
Dixie. See Success
Dozier, Lieutenant William G.
    127, 163
Drain, Acting Master's Mate
    George 39, 40, 42, 165

Duncan, Lieutenant J.M. 19, 90, 105

DuPont, Admiral Samuel F. 20, 52, 74, 90, 159, 167

Dyer, Joseph 139

E

Eastman, Lieutenant Commander T.H. 93

Edward's Ferry, North Carolina 127

Elwell, Master's Mate A. 76, 77

Emanuel, Major William P. 50, 58, 59, 71–74, 105, 112, 158, 162, 167

Emma 90, 159

F

Fair Play 88, 157

Fifteenth Army Corps 134

Fifteenth Illinois Cavalry 134

First Military District 32, 48, 103, 156

First South Carolina Infantry 147

Florence, South Carolina 134, 136

Florida 92

Fort Alston 15, 17

Fort Campbell 37

Fort Caswell 37, 42

Fort Clark 37

Fort Fisher 31, 44

Fort Hatteras 37

Fort Randall 14, 31, 32, 34–40, 42–45, 47, 62, 67, 72, 100, 106, 155, 156, 164–66

Fort Shaw 37

Fort Ward 14, 34, 68, 83, 156

Fort Washington 142

Fort Wool 116, 118, 119, 122

Fourth South Carolina Cavalry 68, 72–74, 112, 167

Fourth South Carolina Infantry 113, 170

Frazier's Point 13, 56, 103, 107, 110, 112, 115, 122, 161, 164, 172

G

Gaillard, Captain Christopher 51

Gaillard's Light Artillery 51, 60, 116, 173

Gainey, Ensign James 39

General Ripley 91

George Chisolm 95, 169

Georgetown, South Carolina 11, 13, 14, 17–20, 23, 24, 31, 32, 34–36, 44, 47–50, 54–56, 60, 62, 63, 67–69, 71, 72, 74, 75, 81, 85–93, 95, 96, 98–107, 113, 116–18, 124–28, 131–34, 139, 141, 142, 144–47, 150, 155–59, 161, 162, 166, 167, 169, 170–72, 174

Georgetown Artillery 86

Georgetown County 35, 159

German Artillery 114, 116, 117, 147, 171, 173, 174

Gillespie, Captain T.F. 34

Golden Liner 71, 75, 94, 102, 166, 167

Gore, Lieutenant T.W. 34

Greensboro, North Carolina 134

Gregory, Acting Master Samuel 78, 80

Gregory, Sam, Jr. 78

H

Hagley Plantation 86, 156

Halleck, General Henry 143

Hardee, General William J. 133, 143, 173, 174

Harllee, General W.W. 87, 127, 128

Harllee, Lieutenant R.Z. 87

Harrison, Captain H.K. 78, 95

Harrison, Commander N.B. 130

Hatch, General John Porter 81, 172

Hazard, John 148

Hebert, General Louis 37

Henning, Captain James G. 86, 156

Hero 42, 92

Hilton Head, South Carolina 32, 35, 48, 103, 156, 157

Home 37

Horry County 14, 31, 35, 47, 107, 155, 178

Hughes, Commander A.K. 61, 166

Hunter, Flag Officer William 135

Hunter, General Daniel 48

J

James Bailey 36, 42, 163, 164

Johnson, Lieutenant Oscar 131, 135, 172, 175

Johnston, General Joseph 135, 145, 175

Jones, Major General Sam 116

Jordan, General Thomas 109, 115, 133

Joseph 50, 105

K

Kate Hale. See Success

Kennedy, Lieutenant Ely 77, 94

Kirk's Rangers 116, 173

Klatte, Lieutenant Hermann 116, 117, 174

L

LaBruce, John 54, 69

LaBruce and Ward saltworks 54, 55, 61, 68, 69, 162

Lachicotte, Lieutenant Philip R. 93

Ladson's Bluff 60

Laurel Hill 14, 47, 56, 65, 161, 178

LeBleux, Lieutenant Louis F. 13

Lee, Captain F.D. 13

Lee, General Robert E. 13, 14, 18, 23, 25, 68, 156, 159, 175

Lee, Master Charles W. 98

Lenud's Ferry 60

Le Roy, Commander William 88–90

Litchfield, Captain J. 34, 156

Litchfield Beach, South Carolina 95

Little River, South Carolina 11, 13, 14, 31, 32, 34–36, 38, 42–44, 47, 48, 61–63, 67, 69, 73, 75, 77, 81, 86, 89, 92, 97, 100, 102, 103, 106, 125, 134, 139, 155–57, 160, 162–66, 170, 171, 174

Lotus 93, 164

Louisa 51, 90, 159

Lowry, Lieutenant H.B 52

Lucy Holmes 90, 159

M

Magill, Dr. Joseph 56

Mallory, Stephen R. 126, 127, 161, 163

Manigault, Colonel Arthur Middleton 14, 18, 19, 21, 23, 32, 48, 49, 60, 86, 87, 103, 104, 112, 155, 156, 158, 177, 179

Margaret and Jessie 95, 168

Mars Bluff Navy Yard 99, 113, 115, 126–28, 131, 133, 135, 138, 161, 163, 169, 170, 172

Mary Stewart 90
Matthews, Lieutenant E.O. 118
Mayrant's Bluff 56, 60, 69, 107,
    109, 110, 112, 144, 161,
    163, 164
McGrath, Seaman Patrick 146
Means, Lieutenant Edward J. 99,
    128
Melchers, Captain Franz 114, 116
Mero, Ensign William 62
Miller, Engineer James A. 146
Montgomery, Alabama 127
Morgan, Lieutenant Van
    Rensselaer 128
Morrill, Captain J.T. 87
Murrells Inlet, South Carolina 11,
    13, 14, 32, 34, 43, 47, 54,
    61–63, 67–69, 71–81, 83,
    86, 89, 92–96, 114, 139,
    156, 161, 162, 166–72

N

Nicolai I 43, 166
Nineteenth South Carolina
    Cavalry 101
Ninth Illinois Infantry 134
Norfolk Navy Yard 126
Northeastern Railroad bridge 35,
    51, 91, 104, 160
North Inlet 20, 87, 89, 96, 98, 99,
    157, 170
North Island 13–15, 17–20, 26,
    49, 52, 58, 68, 85, 87, 91,
    93, 99, 102, 103, 105, 106,
    156, 160, 164, 171, 172
North Island Lighthouse 13, 15,
    17, 19–21, 26, 49, 98, 105
North Santee. See Treaty
North Santee Mounted Rifles 155
Nowell's Point 60

O

Orah Peck 91, 160
Ordinance of Secession 12
Osceola 18, 87, 156
Ost, Charles 36
Oven Bluff, Alabama 127

P

Pathfinder 92
Patrick Henry 131
Pawleys Island, South Carolina 7,
    15, 20, 86, 91, 98, 156, 172
Pee Dee River 11, 14, 35, 48,
    99, 100, 103, 104, 126–28,
    132–34, 139, 174
Pemberton, General John 19, 25,
    48, 55, 56, 59, 60, 61, 68,
    69, 103, 104, 106, 107, 127,
    158, 160–62, 168
Pennell, Master I.A. 61–63, 98
Pickens, Govenor Francis 107
Pinckney, Captain Thomas 51
Porter, Acting Naval Constructor
    John L. 128, 163
Port Royal 13, 20, 93, 164
Prentiss, Commander George A.
    19, 20, 25, 50, 52, 54, 68,
    69, 90, 105, 106, 160
Price, Second Lieutenant J.R. 135
Prince of Wales 18, 87
Proclamation of Blockade 156

Q

Queen of the Wave 93, 102, 165

R

Racoe, Engineer Fred W. 148
Rains, Brigadier General Gabriel
    146, 148
Randall, Captain Thomas 34

Richmond, Virginia 127, 134

Richmond Hill 14, 47

Ripley, General Roswell 19, 104, 108, 158, 160

Robertson, Private Lemuel 96

Rose 20, 98, 99, 102, 172

Rouquie, Lieutenant Stephen A. 147, 172

Rouse, Lieutenant Colonel R.A. 113, 170

Rover 76, 77, 94, 102, 168

S

Saffold, Georgia 127

Sampit River 11, 14, 48, 103

Sands, Captain Benjamin F. 40

Santee Rivers 11, 13, 14, 21, 23, 32, 48–51, 60, 61, 68, 89, 90, 93, 95, 98, 103, 105, 118, 144, 156, 158–60, 163, 165, 169, 171

Savage, Commander Hugh H. 39

Savannah, Georgia 143

Scotia 97, 171

Seabrook 51, 89, 158

Second South Carolina Artillery 60, 74, 109, 114, 163, 167, 171

Selma, Alabama 127

Seventh Illinois Infantry 134

Seventh South Carolina Cavalry 68, 112, 114, 171

Seventh South Carolina Infantry 34

Sherman, General William T. 52, 116, 133–35, 143, 145, 173, 175

Shreveport, Louisiana 127

Singleton's Swash 47, 61, 63, 65, 69

Slocum, General H.W. 134

Smith, Ensign George 39

South Atlantic Blockading Squadron 76, 141, 168

South Island 13, 14, 20, 21, 23, 30, 51, 68, 102, 103, 105, 106

Sparkman's Plantation 47, 58, 91, 162

Stellwagen, Captain H.S. 101, 174

Stono River 54

Success 73, 89, 158

Sue 71, 93, 166

Sullivan's Island, South Carolina 71

Swann, Lieutenant R.P. 115, 116

T

Taber's Point 60

Tenth South Carolina Regiment 17, 21, 23, 34, 87, 104, 147, 157

Third South Carolina Infantry 113, 170

Thomson, Second Lieutenant Ruffin 131

Tilghman's Point 32, 46

Tillson, Ensign Myron 76, 77, 94

Trapier, Brigadier General James Heyward 60, 63, 71, 76, 77, 79, 107–10, 112–17, 119, 124, 128, 131, 133, 134, 162–64, 170, 171, 173

Treaty 51, 55, 58, 69, 85, 90–92, 128, 159, 161, 162

Tucker, Captain John H. 74, 87, 90, 112, 114, 157, 167, 171

Twenty-first Battalion Georgia Cavalry 74, 77, 78, 94–96, 114, 167, 170, 171

Twenty-first South Carolina Regiment 104, 158

Twenty-ninth Missouri Mounted Infantry 134
Twenty-sixth South Carolina Regiment 68

U

USS *Albatross* 19, 21, 25, 49–51, 68, 90, 91, 105, 159, 160
USS *Aries* 96, 97, 170
USS *Baltimore* 143
USS *Bat* 133
USS *Canandaigua* 130, 132, 173
USS *Catalpa* 100, 101, 145, 174
USS *Chenango* 100, 101, 145
USS *Chocura* 40, 71, 73, 94, 167
USS *Cimarron* 61, 98, 166, 171
USS *Clover* 100, 145, 148
USS *Conemaugh* 74, 93, 94, 165, 167
USS *Connecticut* 97, 98, 171
USS *Dacotah* 40, 165
USS *Daffodil* 80, 96, 169
USS *Dai Ching* 95, 169
USS *Darlington* 128
USS *E.B. Hale* 51, 91, 160
USS *Ethan Allen* 61, 62, 80, 96, 98, 169, 171, 172
USS *Fernandina* 35, 157
USS *Flambeau* 74, 75, 100, 145, 167
USS *Fulton* 95, 168
USS *Gem of the Sea* 18, 20, 50, 55, 58, 69, 87–91, 157–59, 161
USS *George Mangham* 80, 96, 169
USS *Geranium* 80, 96, 100, 145, 169
USS *Harvest Moon* 47, 100, 102, 139–51, 153, 171–73, 175
USS *Henry Andrew* 91
USS *Housatonic* 143, 144, 170, 171
USS *Howquah* 95, 168
USS *Keystone State* 88–90, 95, 158, 159, 168
USS *Maratanza* 38, 73, 164, 167

USS *Marblehead* 54, 171
USS *Matthew Vassar* 37, 39, 40, 42, 43, 71, 72, 77, 92, 93, 165, 166
USS *Mingoe* 100, 101, 117, 132, 133, 145, 148, 174
USS *Monitor* 37, 144
USS *Montgomery* 96, 140, 170
USS *Monticello* 36, 44, 61, 69, 71, 72, 74, 92–94, 100, 160, 163, 166, 167, 174
USS *Mount Vernon* 36, 88, 92, 157, 160
USS *Mystic* 36, 92, 160
USS *Nansemond* 95, 168
USS *Nipsic* 80, 81, 96, 100, 145, 169, 170
USS *Norwich* 19, 21, 49, 50, 90, 105, 159
USS *Ottawa* 77, 168
USS *Pawnee* 99, 100, 101, 132, 145, 148, 174
USS *Penobscot* 36, 92, 160
USS *Perry* 78–80, 95, 169
USS *Planter* 128
USS *Pocahontas* 55, 58, 91, 92, 161, 162
USS *Potomska* 115, 173
USS *Quaker City* 93, 165
USS *Sanford* 80, 96, 169
USS *Sebago* 93, 109, 163, 164
USS *Sonoma* 100, 145
USS *State of Georgia* 92, 165
USS *Sweetbriar* 100, 145
USS *T.A. Ward* 76, 77, 78, 94, 168
USS *Victoria* 36, 40, 42, 43, 92, 160, 163–66
USS *Violet* 71
USS *Wamsutta* 20, 98, 99, 172
USS *Western World* 51, 55, 69, 91, 160, 161

V

Vaught, Peter 61, 65, 98, 162
Vaught's saltworks 38, 43, 61, 63,
      162, 171
Vesta 97, 170
Vicksburg, Mississippi 59, 168
Volante 54, 91, 160

W

Waccamaw Light Artillery 17, 34,
      54, 56, 58, 68, 74, 93, 104,
      112, 115, 156, 162, 164,
      165, 167, 172
Waccamaw River 11, 13, 14, 19,
      48, 50, 54, 56, 86, 90, 101,
      103, 106, 115, 156, 159,
      160, 161, 174
Wachesaw Plantation 65
Wachesaw Riflemen 68, 156
Wanklin, Second Assistant
      Engineer Henry 98
Ward, Joshua John 54, 68, 69
Warley, Captain Frederick F. 60,
      109, 112, 163, 164
Warren, Captain Joshua 143
Warren, Ensign E.R. 98
Wateree Mounted Riflemen 61
Weenee 91
Welles, Secretary of the Navy
      Gideon 52, 77, 80
Werden, Commander Reed 74,
      75, 167
Wheeler, Captain 52
Wheeler, General Joe 134
White, Major William Capers 17,
      34, 68, 156, 162
White, Major William P. 96, 170
Whitehall, North Carolina 127
Williams, Colonel Ruben 134
Wilmington, North Carolina 31,
      44, 88, 95–97, 117, 157

Wilmington and Manchester line
      railroad bridge 126
Windsor Plantation 107
Winslow, Executive Officer W.H.
      62
Winyah Bay 11, 13, 14, 17, 19,
      20, 21, 23, 25, 26, 31, 34,
      43, 48, 49, 52, 56, 60, 61,
      67–69, 86, 89–92, 96, 98–
      100, 103, 105–07, 113–15,
      117, 126, 127, 131–33, 139,
      144, 145, 147, 149, 150,
      153, 159–63, 172
Witherspoon, Colonel J.H. 113,
      170
Withers Swash 43, 62, 63, 69, 98,
      172

Y

Yates, Lieutenant Colonel Joseph
      71–74, 166, 167
Yazoo City, Mississippi 127
Young, Second Lieutenant
      Thomas 96

About the Author

D r. Rick Simmons was born and raised in South Carolina, and during the course of his education, he attended Clemson University, Coastal Carolina University and the University of South Carolina, where he completed his PhD in 1997. He currently lives in Louisiana with his wife, Sue, and his children, Courtenay and Cord, though he still spends a portion of the summer at his family home in Pawleys Island, South Carolina. He is the holder of the George K. Anding Endowed Professorship  at Louisiana Tech University, where he is currently the director of the Center for Academic and Professional Development.

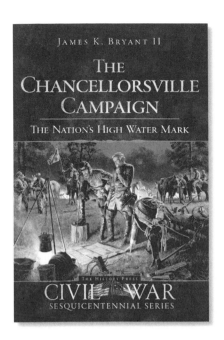

JAMES K. BRYANT II

THE CHANCELLORSVILLE CAMPAIGN

The Nation's High Water Mark

CIVIL WAR
SESQUICENTENNIAL SERIES

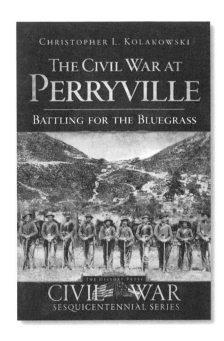

CHRISTOPHER L. KOLAKOWSKI

THE CIVIL WAR AT PERRYVILLE

Battling for the Bluegrass

CIVIL WAR
SESQUICENTENNIAL SERIES

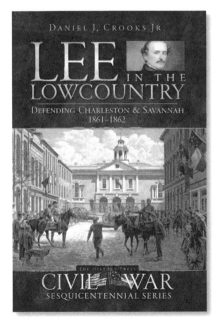

DANIEL J. CROOKS JR.

LEE IN THE LOWCOUNTRY

Defending Charleston & Savannah 1861–1862

CIVIL WAR
SESQUICENTENNIAL SERIES

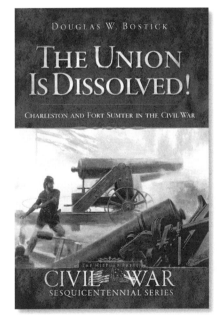

DOUGLAS W. BOSTICK

THE UNION IS DISSOLVED!

Charleston and Fort Sumter in the Civil War

CIVIL WAR
SESQUICENTENNIAL SERIES

THE HISTORY PRESS

CIVIL WAR

SESQUICENTENNIAL SERIES

The History Press Civil War Sesquicentennial Series offers thoroughly researched, accessible accounts of important aspects of the war rarely covered outside the academic realm. Explore a range of topics from influential but lesser-known battles and campaigns to the local and regional impact of the war's figures—whether celebrated generals or common soldiers. Each book is crafted in a way that Civil War enthusiasts and casual readers alike will enjoy.

Books in this series from The History Press include:

The Chancellorsville Campaign
978.1.59629.594.0 * 6 x 9 * 160pp * $19.99

The Civil War at Perryville
978.1.59629.672.5 * 6 x 9 * 192pp * $21.99

Lee in the Lowcountry
978.1.59629.589.6 * 6 x 9 * 128pp * $19.99

The Union Is Dissolved!
978.1.59629.573.5 * 6 x 9 * 128pp * $19.99

Visit us at
www.historypress.net